*f*P

YOUR 15th CLUB

The Inner Secret to Great Golf

DR. BOB ROTELLA

WITH BOB CULLEN

FREE PRESS
New York   London   Toronto   Sydney

FREE PRESS
A Division of Simon & Schuster, Inc.
1230 Avenue of the Americas
New York, NY 10020

First Free Press hardcover edition May 2008

FREE PRESS and colophon are trademarks of Simon & Schuster, Inc.

For information about special discounts for bulk purchases,
please contact Simon & Schuster Special Sales at 1-800-456-6798
or business@simonandschuster.com

DESIGNED BY ERICH HOBBING

Manufactured in the United States of America

1   3   5   7   9   10   8   6   4   2

Library of Congress Cataloging-in-Publication Data
Rotella, Robert J.
Your 15th club : the inner secret to great golf / by Bob Rotella with
Robert Cullen.
p. cm.
1. Golf—Psychological aspects. I. Cullen, Robert, 1949- II. Title.
III. Title: Your fifteenth club.
GV979.P75R678 2008
796.35201'9—dc22   2008000686

ISBN-13: 978-1-4165-6796-7
ISBN-10:   1-4165-6796-8

I dedicate this book to:
Dr. Frank Luth,
for giving me a chance to teach children with special needs
at Brandon Training School;

Coaches Frank Bizzarro and Jim Parmalee,
for giving me opportunities to coach high school basketball
at Mt. St. Joseph Academy and E.O. Smith High School;

Coaches Nate Osur and Glen Thiel,
for giving me a chance to coach lacrosse, at the University
of Connecticut and the University of Virginia, respectively;

The University of Virginia,
for giving me the chance to start and direct its
doctoral degree program in applied sports psychology;

And to the staffs at the
Golf Digest Instructional Schools and *Golf Digest* magazine,
for giving me my first chance to work with golfers
thirty years ago.

My thanks to all.

Contents

Your 15th Club

The Inner Secret to Great Golf

Foreword

Your 15th Club is about believing in yourself when you play golf. It's about self-confidence rather than swing confidence. It's about seeing yourself as a winner. It's about trusting yourself when things are falling apart as well as when they're coming together. It's about letting yourself go low when you have a chance to go low, about letting yourself win when you have a chance to win, about scoring and getting the ball in the hole regardless of how you are hitting the ball.

This book is about respecting your game and your talent. It's about winning the battle within yourself. It's about never wandering and never wavering during a round. It's about never giving in and never giving up. It's about having pride in a strong, tough mind. It's about loving the challenge of playing the game.

I'm going to be demanding of you. I'm going to ask you to take an honest look at the self no one else knows. I'm going to ask you to face the challenge of the game and decide to believe in yourself. I'm going to ask for a commitment to a regimen. This regimen will allow you to develop the sort of mind that wins in golf—and to maintain it.

In return, you will find new joy in the game you love.

The commitment I speak of is not easy. Not everyone is up to the challenge. But if you think you are up to it, you're just the sort of person I love to work with.

Welcome.

1.

Confidence—

Plain and Unvarnished

Padraig Harrington helped crystallize my reason for writing this book. Padraig is a very thoughtful, analytical man. He's been a client and a friend for ten years, but I wouldn't call myself his mental coach or his sports psychologist. Padraig and I have conversations. My role usually amounts to listening to the things he's figured out and nodding my head. I learn as much from Padraig as he learns from me.

Not long ago, Padraig mentioned that he recommends the book I wrote in 1994, *Golf Is Not a Game of Perfect*, to the people he plays with, including fellow pros. I was intrigued, and not just because word of mouth is the best advertising. I know that Padraig is a friendly, generous fellow, but I also know that he's a competitor down to the bone. I know he thought *Golf Is Not a Game of Perfect* had helped him, so I was curious as to why he'd recommend the book to players who were trying to take away what he has—the top ranking among European players.

"I'm not worried if someone reads it," he said when I asked him about it. "That's fine. It's an easy read. They'll enjoy it. They'll gain from it. But they won't get the real benefit unless they live it—and that's the hard part. So I can tell my competitors to go and read *Golf Is Not a Game of Perfect* and I know I'm not giving anything up unless they actually do the work."

Padraig's statement meshed with thoughts I'd been having for a while. As a sports psychologist, I go to my clients as often as they come to me, especially after I've been working with them for some time. Since many of them are tournament golfers, I see them at tournament venues—generally on the putting green or the practice range. Players who have worked with me often need only a quick conversation to clear up a specific question and prepare their minds for a competitive round.

Frequently, as I move down the range or around the green, I chat with players who aren't clients, at least not in the traditional sense. They may not have worked with me personally, but they've read *Golf Is Not a Game of Perfect* or another of my books on golf and the mind. They're generally complimentary. Increasingly, though, in recent years, I've heard something like this:

"Doc, I read *Golf Is Not a Game of Perfect* eight years ago, and it really helped me. I was able to play my best golf in the clutch, coming down the stretch. In fact, I won a couple of times right after I read it. But lately, it doesn't seem to be working as well. I think you ought to write another book."

This is that book. But it's not going to be another iteration of *Golf Is Not a Game of Perfect* or any of its sequels.

I'm afraid I may have been inadvertently misleading in those books. It's not that they contain any misinformation. They don't. When I wrote *Golf Is Not a Game of Perfect*, I conveyed the truth about the mental side of golf under pressure, truth I'd learned working in several sports and field-tested over fifteen years with professional golfers. Those years of field-testing have now stretched close to thirty, and I'm more convinced than ever about what works for golfers. You've got to follow your dreams. You will become what you think about yourself. You've got to train your swing, then trust it. You've got to accept the mistakes that inevitably happen on the golf course. You've got to manage your temper as well as the course. You've got to fall in love with the short game, the part of golf that most heavily impacts scoring. Above all, you must be confident.

But in my previous books, as Padraig and other pros have helped me realize, I failed to stress one very important aspect of the mental game. I may have left the impression that mastering the mental game was like riding a bicycle, something you could learn and then always be able to do.

It's not. The fact is that having the sort of mind that stands up to clutch situations and wins golf tournaments is much more like having a fit body. Yes, you have to work to reach a desired level of fitness. But, once you're there, you have to work to keep it. Your body will slide back into softness and weakness if you don't continue to work out. Your mental game, too, will become soft and weak if you don't continue to monitor it and work on it. That's the work Padraig was talking about.

This, I think, explains the statements I've heard from players who say that an earlier book helped them for a while but doesn't seem to work as well anymore. It's because those books didn't make it clear enough that for golfers, having a strong mind in the clutch is part of a process. While the books were fresh in their memories, these players were unconsciously engaged in a process that strengthened their minds. They came through under pressure and played the sort of golf they had always sensed they could play. But golf is a little bit like the ocean's waves. Just as the waves will work relentlessly to erode the dunes at the top of a beach, golf will work relentlessly to erode a player's confidence. Just as beach towns have to work constantly and vigilantly to strengthen and protect their dunes, golfers must work to maintain their confidence and the strength of their minds.

Maybe, like the players I sometimes meet on Tour, you read *Golf Is Not a Game of Perfect* a dozen years ago and find that your mind seems to work less effectively now than it did right after you read it. If so, it's not because that book is any less valid. It's because I failed to emphasize that you need to commit yourself to a constant process of strengthening your mind. It's as if you hired a personal trainer a dozen years ago and worked with him until you could bench-press 200 pounds and run a mile in six minutes. But the trainer left town without giving you a workout plan to sustain that level of performance. For that omission, I apologize.

The book you're holding will correct that deficiency. Like my previous books, it will have a few stories and anecdotes about players. I hope it will be, in places, entertaining to read. But I will do a bit less storytelling in this book, because I want to emphasize the process of developing and maintaining a strong mental game. I want you to be confronted on every page, not with stories about other golfers, but with things you need to know and do to strengthen your mind so that you can play your best golf in the clutch. I want reading this book to be like sitting with me in my basement in Virginia, where I counsel players, or talking with me on the practice range at a Tour event. I don't often tell stories in those settings. I tell players what I think they need to hear. I give it to them plain and unvarnished.

Sometimes it can be hard for golfers to hear this. People want quick results. I've yet to see someone try to sell a diet program that will give you the body you want—a year from now. The automobile companies don't advise you to save your money and budget carefully if you want a top-of-the-line luxury model. They all know people want instant gratification. I'm not promising immediate results in this book. I'm talking about a process that will steadily strengthen your mind and keep it strong for as long as you stay on it. But that doesn't mean you'll win tomorrow if you read the book tonight.

There's another reason why the things I am going to tell you in this book may not appeal to everyone. For some reason, in our culture, it's a lot easier for many people to admit they're working on their golf swings than it is to admit they're working on their thinking. People will go for years to golf professionals for lessons on their mechanics. They'll spend weeks on drills that are designed to improve their swings and groove good movements. They'll chat with their friends on the practice range, sometimes a bit too much, about the things they're doing to make their swings better. Or they might go see a fitness trainer and get a new stretching routine. They'll drop to the ground and twist like a yoga master at the first sign someone's interested in seeing a demonstration of what they're doing. And I'm glad they will. I'm the first to say that success in golf is a product of both body and mind. If you want to be the best golfer you can be, you've got to master certain physical fundamentals.

But if players are eager to talk about the changes they're making in their mechanics, why do they shy away from talking about a mental overhaul? On a logical level, this doesn't make sense to me. Why should someone show you, without embarrassment, a drill that requires him to hit balls standing on one foot like a flamingo and yet be reluctant to discuss the fifteen minutes he spends at night visualizing success? I don't know. If I told people that they could win a major championship by spending an hour a night walking across a bed of hot coals, many of them would immediately start taking off their shoes and socks. But the thought of spending that same hour working on their psyche doesn't appeal to them. Maybe it's because a physical or mechanical flaw seems to be a little farther from the core of a person's identity. A thinking flaw strikes closer to who we are.

This, I believe, is why a lot of golfers hit a wall when they reach the stage where their mechanics are no longer the primary obstacle. They've put in lots of hours learning to strike the ball well. Whether their goal is winning major championships or getting to a single-digit handicap, they have the physical skills to do it. But they start to lose traction. Often, they regress. They can't admit to themselves that it's their thinking that's holding them back. They don't commit themselves to a program to strengthen their minds. They fail to change.

So the first thing I'm asking you to do as you read this book is to be honest with yourself. Is your present way of thinking consistent with the level of golf you'd like to play? Does it help you in the clutch, or does it handicap you? Does it enable you to find out how good you could be?

And do you dare to change it?

2.

The 15th Club

It would be fascinating if, someday, either Tiger Woods or Annika Sorenstam were to give an interview in which he or she spoke about confidence with complete candor. It's not going to happen. Both of them are too smart about the media and our culture to reveal themselves so completely. But it would be both helpful and revealing if they did.

Tiger and Annika are the best clutch golfers of our time. That's different from saying they've got the best physical tools in the game. They both have admirable and abundant physical skills, skills that they've honed through years of dedicated practice. But they're not flawless. Annika's putting has never been consistently brilliant. Tiger hits so many crooked shots with his driver that I sometimes think he's got the yips with that club. And even the physical strengths of their games are not unmatched. You can go to the practice area at any PGA or LPGA Tour event and see players who hit the ball as long or as straight, who wedge it just as close, who sink as many putts.

What separates these players from the competition, I believe, is their confidence. It's what I am going to call their 15th club. Deep inside, they both feel they will beat anyone who tees it up against them. That confidence is what enables them to play the way they do in the clutch. Too many of their competitors don't think that way.

When I visualize a player's 15th club, my mind goes back to my boyhood, when I was a caddie in Rutland, Vermont. I used to hear a lot of players back then, especially fellow caddies, talk about a favorite club. Maybe it was because manufacturing tolerances weren't so precise back then and clubs from the same set might have appreciably different feels. Maybe it was because people very often scraped together a set of clubs from hand-me-downs and castoffs, and one or two of the clubs in the bag felt better to them than the others. You don't hear so much about favorite clubs anymore, probably because modern clubs are made better and golfers tend to buy them in complete sets.

But back then, lots of golfers had a particular club they felt especially comfortable with. It might have been an 8-iron they liked to use for every shot within 130 yards of the green. Maybe it was an old brassie, or 3-wood, that they just knew would put the ball in the fairway on a tight hole. More often than not, the favorite club did in fact work better than the other clubs in the bag.

I don't think this happened just because those players' favorite clubs were physically better made or better suited to them. I think it was because laying their fingers around the grip of their favorite club produced a feeling of calm confidence. They didn't just hope to hit the ball where they were looking. They didn't just want to hit it there. They expected to. That made a huge difference.

When I think of your 15th club, I'm obviously not thinking of an actual club. I know the rules allow you to carry only fourteen. I'm thinking of that feeling of calm confidence, that expectation that you'll hit the ball where you want it to go. That's what I want you to get from this book. It's a feeling you'll be able to call on in any golfing situation, no matter how stressful. It's the feeling Tiger and Annika have on Sunday afternoons.

If Tiger or Annika were to be completely revealing, he or she would probably say something like, "I'm the best in the world—heck, the best that's ever been. If I show up and play my normal game, everyone else is competing for second place. That's how good I am."

They don't say that because they understand that doing so would antagonize a large portion of the public. Muhammad Ali was hated when he predicted the round in which he'd knock out opponents. Joe Namath was reviled for guaranteeing that his Jets would beat the Baltimore Colts in Super Bowl III. Their popularity survived because, ultimately, they backed up what they said. But expressing too much confidence in our culture is considered a sign of boorish arrogance. So smart athletes, like Tiger and Annika, learn to keep their true feelings private. They may even exhibit a facade of humility that masks their inner arrogance so they don't antagonize people. I can understand why they do it, though they would not antagonize me if they were to let the public see the true extent of their confidence. I admire that sort of confidence in an athlete. But I'm unusual.

Our culture has a peculiar, contradictory attitude toward confidence. We try to instill a certain amount of it. Smart Little League coaches are forever telling kids, "You can do it." So are smart math teachers. Later in life, so are sales directors. But our approval of confidence and our effort to instill it go only so far. No one wants a kid who's "cocky," "arrogant," "full of himself," or any of the myriad other synonyms we have for overconfidence. Maybe it's because parents or coaches are afraid they'll lose control over a child or an athlete if the child gets "too" confident. Maybe they're afraid of losing their own role as the ultimate authority in the child's life. Maybe they're afraid that a child who's "too" confident will not want to practice or study. Whatever the reason, our culture is quick to turn on someone who goes beyond what is deemed an acceptable level of confidence. There's an old proverb that tells us that "the nail that sticks up gets pounded down."

If Tiger and Annika were to publicly express the true level of their confidence, they'd doubtless feel that hammer.

I'm not advocating braggadocio. I don't appreciate someone who loudly tells the world how good he or she is any more than most people do. But I do admire the private arrogance that characterizes Tiger and Annika. That private, inner arrogance is something I want you to feel comfortable with.

In golf, as in many endeavors, there is no such thing as too much confidence. I have never had a player come to me and say, "You know, Doc, the reason I came apart in the clutch in my last tournament was that I was too confident." I suppose it is hypothetically possible to be overconfident. You could conceivably have a player who doesn't do enough practice because he's overconfident. You could have a player who tries a long carry over water, longer than he can manage, because he's overconfident. But only hypothetically. I can assure you that in thirty years of working with professional golfers, I've yet to have such a client. But nearly every day, I work with someone whose problem is lack of confidence.

I want you to develop the same sort of inner arrogance that Tiger and Annika have. If you're afraid you'll be perceived by others as obnoxious, don't worry. You need never let anyone else know how confident you really are. You can keep it to yourself. But I hope that after you've read this book and worked on the regimen it prescribes, you'll be an inwardly arrogant golfer, calm and sure of yourself in all situations.

When a player lacks this inner arrogance, the deficiency shows up in clutch situations. I define clutch situations in various ways. For my professional clients, it can be the last nine holes of a major championship where they're in contention. For some of my amateur clients, it can be the finals of the club championship. For others, it might be just a member-guest with a boss or that moment when they walk onto the 18th tee and someone tells them that if they par the final hole, they'll break 80—for the first time.

Players with sufficient confidence handle these situations. They know that success doesn't mean that they must play absolutely flawless golf. If Tiger thought that success required him to drive the ball into the fairway every time he got into contention, how many tournaments would he have won? Players with confidence believe that even without flawless golf, they'll find a way to win. Consequently, they're patient. Though they feel the same physical symptoms of nerves that other players feel, they don't let the butterflies rattle them. They attach the same low level of importance to every shot they hit. They play with the same quiet focus they have in practice. They stick with the same proven shotmaking routines that got them into the clutch situation to begin with. Quite often, though not always, of course, they win.

Players who lack confidence respond to clutch situations in exactly the opposite way. They forget, for instance, that success doesn't mean perfection. If it did, would Angel Cabrera have won the 2007 U.S. Open after bogeying two of the last three holes? They strive for perfection. In doing so, they make themselves tight. They try harder. They invest more importance in certain shots than those shots truly deserve. They may panic at the onset of nervous symptoms. Instead of remembering all the times they've accomplished the tasks that stand before them, they remember the times they've failed. They abandon their routines. Maybe they take so many practice strokes that their minds start to wander. Maybe they abandon practice strokes altogether and start doing everything more quickly than they should. They stop playing the golf that got them into the clutch situation. They walk off the course feeling that they've choked.

They may even realize that they failed for lack of confidence. But when I explore this point, I usually find that they have no understanding of what confidence really is, how to develop it, or how to sustain it.

Players frequently tell me, "When I have all the parts of my game where I want them, then I'll be confident." That is, on the day when they're driving it long and straight, hitting their irons right at the flag, and making every putt they look at, they'll believe they can win.

I call this "swing confidence." Sad to say, it's a chimera. No matter how talented a player is and no matter how much he practices, he will have all of his mechanics in order about as often as you can expect a quick, unfettered drive to work in Los Angeles. That's the nature of golf. The mechanics are complex. A lot can go wrong. Something usually does. If you base your confidence on having all your mechanics fall into place, you'll lose that confidence as soon as you hit an imperfect shot. Ben Hogan used to say that he considered himself to be doing well when he hit two or three perfect shots in a round. If that's all Hogan could expect, how long do you think swing confidence will last the next time you're in a clutch situation?

Swing confidence almost never pulls you through in the clutch. A different kind of confidence does. It comes from within a player, not from the way he strikes the ball on a given day. Let's call it real confidence. The player with real confidence believes that even if he's having only an average day, he can still get the ball in the hole better than the other guy. He doesn't have to hit the ball perfectly. He can still score. He can still win.

When I explain this to players, I often hear a reaction along the lines of, "Well, if I had Tiger's talent, and if I'd been winning like Tiger has since childhood, and if I'd been raised by parents who were always telling me I was destined to do great things, then I'd have real confidence, like Tiger's. But I didn't."

A player has to abandon every part of this rationalization if he wants to become a confident golfer.

First, if you want to play well in the clutch you've got to like your talent more than you like anyone else's. If you like someone else's talent more than yours, you might as well not enter the tournament.

You might object, "But it's obvious that so-and-so has more talent than I do. Look how much farther he hits the ball."

All I can tell you is that hitting the ball a long way, while it's desirable, is hardly the most important talent a golfer needs to bring to a tournament. What about accuracy? What about a short game? What about putting? And, finally, what about the strength of will that a player possesses? That's not immediately visible on the practice range, but it may well be the single most important talent a golfer can possess. Did Tiger or Phil Mickelson take a look at Bubba Watson, who hits it longer than they do, and say, "Well, it's all over for me because someone with more talent has arrived"?

The fact is, you don't know how much talent you have until you play with real confidence. So assume you have the talent it takes to reach the goals you want to reach.

Some players might agree with this idea but still rationalize that if they weren't child prodigies, they simply can't have the confidence of someone who was. There's no doubt that if you were writing a development plan for a champion golfer and you could determine the course of events from infancy on, you'd want that golfer to win early and often. You'd want that player to start with lots of junior championships. You'd then want him to beat players older than he was. You'd want him, at a certain point, to start getting acquainted with successful pros so he could play the occasional friendly round with them and realize that their physical gifts were no better than his. You'd want him, in other words, to grow up the way Jack Nicklaus or Bobby Jones or Tiger Woods did.

But that's not the only path to becoming a confident tournament golfer. Jones, Nicklaus, and Woods are not the only great players. Plenty of our best golfers have been late bloomers. *They* should be the role models for most players.

Consider a player like Fred Funk. He didn't grow up in a

country club family. He wasn't anyone's all-American at the University of Maryland. He went broke in his first effort to play the mini-tours. In his twenties, he supported himself as a golf coach and a newspaper deliveryman. He didn't get out on the PGA Tour until his thirties. He was never a long hitter. But he never stopped believing in himself. His belief sustained a prodigious work ethic. He wore out wedges practicing his short game. And in his forties, he became one of the most successful players in the game. He made the American Ryder Cup and Presidents Cup teams. He won the Players Championship. He's still winning tournaments even as some of the child prodigies of his generation slip into obscurity.

For some reason, it's easier for some players to dismiss the example of a player like Fred Funk and dwell on the fact that they're not Tiger Woods. They've read about the way Earl Woods raised Tiger to be a champion from the cradle. They've read how he told Tiger he'd be a great man. They've read how his mother, Kultida, instilled discipline and toughness in her son. They didn't have that upbringing, they'll say. They just had normal parents who didn't want them to get too cocky.

To begin with, we don't really know all that went on in Tiger's childhood. We have only what Earl Woods and Tiger remember and have chosen to say publicly about it. There were no cameras or recorders in the Woods home or in the car as Kultida Woods drove Tiger to his junior events. So there's no truly scientific way to evaluate Tiger's upbringing or to calculate the impact it had on his ability to play with confidence.

I'll stipulate that Tiger's parents did a fantastic job raising him. They gave him a sense of security at the same time that they challenged him to do great things. They taught him to be disciplined and polite. Not many young people could have the success that Tiger has enjoyed and stay as level-headed and hardworking as Tiger has been.

More important than what his parents did, however, has been what Tiger has done. He bought into his parents' dreams of great achievements and made them his own. Invariably, I find that it's the decisions people make for themselves, not the childhood input of parents and teachers, that determine who they become.

Annika Sorenstam grew up in a family where a girl was expected to be a superb golfer. But that girl was her sister, Charlotta. It was Annika, acting as an individual at the age of twelve, who decided to become the best golfer she could be. Eventually, she far surpassed Charlotta's accomplishments, as well as those of all of her peers. Nowadays, Charlotta teaches at Annika's golf academy.

If you're reading this book, you're old enough to take responsibility for your own thinking. It doesn't matter any longer what your parents did or didn't tell you. It doesn't matter whether they encouraged you or discouraged you. Whatever happened in the past is in the past. It might be slightly helpful. It might be an obstacle you need to overcome. But it's not that important. Your mind is your own. You have it within yourself to develop the confidence you need to see what kind of golfer you can become. You have it within yourself to play your best golf in the clutch. You have it within yourself to develop real confidence.

I am going to show you how.

3.

This Game
Will Beat You Up

Since I spoke in the last chapter about how golf can beat you up, perhaps I ought to make something clear here. I love everything about golf. I love its challenges. I love its beauty. I love its exhilaration. I love it so much that I can come home from a couple of weeks on the road, dead tired after working every daylight hour at a golf course helping players, and wake up the next morning wondering whether my schedule will allow me to get out to the golf course to play that day.

But I know very few players whose love affair with the game runs smoothly. Golf can be cruel. A golfer who loves the game, whose dream is to improve at it, can get lost faster than a tourist in Tokyo. This is why you need a mental regimen. Without one, the game can indeed beat you up. It can sap your confidence. It can leave you standing on a tee somewhere, trees on the left and water on the right, wondering, "What am I doing here?"

This is as true of the elite players on the PGA Tour as it is of amateurs whose swing paths resemble a plate of spaghetti. In fact, it's more true. Your average 16-handicapper, if he accepts playing at that level, is less vulnerable to golf's cruelties than a professional chasing the elusive goal of perfection.

I know this because so many of the players I work with fall into that category. Their skills are extraordinary. They have swings, short games, and putting strokes most amateurs can only dream about. But they're not on the PGA Tour, and they want to be. Or they're on the Tour, but they haven't won. And they want to win. Or they've won on the PGA Tour, maybe many times, but they're not the best. And they want to be.

Such golfers can find the process of improvement very perilous. They are by nature passionate about the game. They understand what it means to make a commitment. What they may not understand is that when you make a commitment to get better, you must work on both your mind and your physical skills. You must try to get better by looking inside yourself as well as outside yourself.

Sometimes, my professional clients decide to get better because they want to please someone else. Maybe they've signed a new endorsement deal. They're going to get paid a handsome sum of money for a period of several years just for using equipment they might have used anyway if they had to go into a pro shop and buy their clubs. Or maybe they're sensitive to what they hear and read in the media. "So-and-so can win the regular events, but he hasn't won a major." "So-and-so hasn't lived up to his potential."

More often, the pressure they put on themselves comes from within. They may have had a couple of seasons that, due to injuries, didn't meet their expectations. Or maybe they're midway through their careers and they reach a time of assessment, and they decide they've got only a limited window in which to fulfill all the dreams they had as boys.

A player like this will typically embark on a campaign to improve his body and his swing. In the world of the very competitive golfer, nothing he reads or hears is as galling as the common observation that "No one is going to outwork Tiger Woods." The type of player I am talking about may not be certain he has Tiger's talent. But he is certain indeed that he is willing to work. He vows to get stronger. He vows to get more flexible. He vows to avoid injury by taking perfect care of himself. He vows to get rid of a wrinkle or two in his mechanics, wrinkles that he believes the very best players do not have. He wants to get his backswing just a little closer to the ideal plane. He wants to shorten the swing just a little bit, to make it more compact and efficient. He wants to modify his impact position. He wants to get rid of that one shot that he thinks has plagued him all through his competitive career. Maybe it's a tendency to block the ball to the right. Maybe it's the occasional snap hook. He will find a teacher who can iron out all of these wrinkles. He decides he is going to show people that he will work as hard as anyone has ever worked. He is excited. He is juiced. He is on a mission.

In the beginning, he really loves the improvement process. He loves coming home exhausted from long hours on the range and in the gym. He's fascinated by the wisdom of the new teachers he's found. It's amazing to him that in his years in golf, he never realized there were alternate theories about the swing. He never knew there were other, slightly different ways to address the ball, altering its position relative to his stance. He never knew there were other ways to envision the backswing, the action of the hands, the core muscles, or the wrists. On the practice range, with his new teacher standing at his side, he starts to hit a few that look exactly like the shot he's always dreamed of hitting. He's going to be longer off the tee and straighter. After a month of dieting and longer workouts, he has the pleasure of ordering a new collection of golf pants, a couple of inches smaller in the waist. His teachers are as enthused as he is about the unlimited potential they see in front of them.

In the beginning, it's okay that the improvements he sees on the range are not always evident in competition. It's understandable that he makes the occasional double and triple bogey, though numbers like that rarely, if ever, got onto his card before. It's understandable that he's hitting the ball in directions he's never hit it before. He's patient.

Besides, in addition to his swing, he's decided to overhaul his short game. He's got a new technique for pitching the ball and a new technique for hitting bunker shots. They're going to give him options around the greens that he never had before. They're also a work in progress.

As time goes by, though, patience thins. Yes, the new swing occasionally produces shots that make the player sigh with pure pleasure. They have the length, the trajectory, and the shape he's always dreamed of. And that pesky shot, the wild hook or the blocked fade, or whatever it was, has pretty much disappeared. On the other hand, the player used to know where he'd miss it if he missed it. Now he doesn't know where his misses are going. And there are more missed shots. He used to be able to play down one side of a hole or the other, knowing that if he missed, the ball would go either left or right. Now he doesn't know where to aim. That sense of doubt starts to erode the other parts of his game. He starts failing to get up and down from places where he used to do it routinely. He doesn't make as many birdie putts as he once did, partly because he has fewer of them and partly because the ones he gets tend to be from farther away.

Missed cuts start to pile up. Writers and broadcasters, so friendly and positive when things were going well, are still friendly. But now the questions begin to be about what's happened to his game and why he's playing so poorly. At first, he brags about how hard he's working and the changes he's making and everyone nods and tries to get the details right. But after a few months, the reporters stop taking notes and rolling tape when he talks about his changes. The only things that roll are their eyes. On the range at a Tour event, the player can feel other eyes watching him. It's as if laser beams were boring into his back. He can hear murmurs. He knows that people—fellow players, other swing coaches, caddies, equipment reps, the entourage of the Tour—are talking about him. They're discussing his changes, and maybe why they're not working, and why they're not right for him. They don't want him to hear, of course, so they lower their voices. He thinks he hears the phrase "poor guy," which no one has ever applied to him in his life.

The player did not, however, become successful by being quick to give up. He persists. It's part of his character, one of his strengths. He works harder. So does his teacher. The teachers who work with professional golfers are a dedicated and intelligent group. They know the golf swing. They also know that their careers depend, in part, on the success of the players they tutor. So when they start working with a well-known player, especially one in a slump, they're ready to spend as much time as it takes to get the player back on track.

Pretty soon, the player and the swing teacher are spending a lot of time together. The swing teacher walks along with the caddie during practice rounds. He's there during the warm-up period before every competitive round. He has dinner with the player at night. Every time the player hits a golf ball, the teacher is there, evaluating the player's alignment, his posture, his grip, his backswing, his plane, and so on. Most teachers nowadays accept the principle that in competition, and as competition nears, it's important that a player stops thinking about mechanics and plays with a trusting mind, thinking about where he wants the ball to go and assuming that his swing will send it there. But it's hard, with so much at stake, to resist a little tweak or two. It's especially hard to shrug your shoulders and say nothing when a player who's paying you to help him turns to you after a shot and asks, "What did I do wrong?"

And that will happen. Players who are going through a self-improvement process tend to become very analytical about their games and their swings. They tend to become very judgmental. They want to pick apart and evaluate every swing. That may not be a bad way to think if you're in the beginning of an improvement plan and you're going to take a couple of months off to change your swing before you enter competition again. It's not a good way to be thinking just before or during competitions. Yet I frequently see players playing practice rounds on the day before a major championship with their swing coaches in tow. They're talking about the mechanics of nearly every shot the player hits. I see coaches tinkering with posture and alignment mere minutes before the player tees off in a tournament round.

The next day, the player opens the tournament with a 78. Every swing he makes seems wooden. The round seems to last forever. By trying very hard to get better, the player has made himself worse. This is the essential cruelty of the game. It's what I hope to help you avoid.

If you pare away the trappings of professional tournament golf and reduce the number of hours involved by a factor of five or ten, this syndrome affects amateurs as well. Maybe the amateur player is tired of shooting in the 80s and wants to play in the 70s. Maybe he wants to win the club championship after a few years of getting beaten in the early rounds. Within the limits of his time and resources, he attacks the problem the same way the pro does. He goes to a golf school. He finds a new pro and takes a series of lessons. Maybe he reads something in a magazine about the latest new swing theory, something like the stack-and-tilt or Natural Golf. He decides to revamp his swing and to go to the gym more often. Initially, he's pumped.

But if it's hard for a pro to make a radical swing change, with all of his talent and all of his practice time, it's doubly so for the amateur. He has less time to work on his game. He has to schedule his lessons; no pro is going to walk with him as he plays practice rounds. The amateur in the midst of a push to improve realizes that for him, the payoff from golf isn't money. It's the camaraderie, the Saturday four-ball matches with his buddies. So he keeps playing in them, trying to play to his handicap while still working on his swing. His buddies may alternately tease him about his new mechanics or offer well-meaning tips and observations (often wrong) about what he's doing.

In that, the amateur is not so different from the pro. You might think that a top-flight professional golfer would know better than to listen to just anyone who wants to offer advice on his golf swing. You would be wrong. You would be wrong especially if this is a player who's not doing as well as he once did, or wants to do. I've never known a player who took a swing tip from the flight attendant on the journey to the tournament, but I've known players who would have been tempted. There are hundreds of people with inside-the-ropes passes at every professional tournament. Most of them know at least something about the golf swing, though only a few know as much as they think they do. With nothing but good intentions, they decide they're going to suggest to good ol' Joe, who's been struggling, that the way they remember him swinging a few years ago, when he was winning, is just a little different from the way they see him swinging now. And they tell him so. Joe should nod coldly and politely and immediately forget everything such people say. But Joe doesn't always do that. It's amazing how often Joe seems to assume that the person giving him the tip never misses a fairway or a six-footer.

It's still worse for the amateur. The members of the average Saturday foursome are much better qualified to practice law, accounting, or taxidermy than to give swing tips. When they do give a tip, it's usually something that they think has helped their swings. That doesn't by any means guarantee it will help the recipient of the tip. But a player who's floundering, whether it's Joe in your foursome or Joe on the Tour, is inclined to listen.

There's nothing wrong with talking about golf techniques. But a player has to remember that working solely on his physical game is like doing leg presses with only the right leg. If you were to do that, you'd eventually start walking with a limp. If you set out to achieve mechanical perfection in golf, but you neglect to develop a mental regimen that nourishes confidence, you'll start listening to the wrong sorts of talk about technique. You'll get lost.

A pro in this situation eventually finds himself feeling emotions opposite to the excited and optimistic ones with which he began his quest to improve. He sits in his hotel room at night wondering why he's doing it all. Why is he traveling and spending money just to miss cuts and get paid nothing? If he's at the age where he's got a wife and children at home, which is frequently the case, he wonders how he can justify spending so much time away from them. He starts feeling guilty about his role as a parent and provider. Especially if he's been at it for a while and has saved enough money to get by on, he starts wondering if he even wants to play anymore.

For the amateur, the financial considerations don't exist. But he or she may have a spouse and a family, and he or she may well wonder if golf is worth the time it requires.

This is often the stage at which someone will pick up the phone and call me.

I get calls from clients who regularly contend in major championships. They play on international teams. Their swings are the envy of many of their fellow pros, to say nothing of the average player. But when they call me, what I often hear is, "I'm terrible. I'm just scared to death. I have no feeling I can play well this week."

I have clients who have won major championships who call me and tell me they are hitting the ball better than anybody they play against—but they're a mess on the greens. They putt very well in practice and good putters tell them they have fine strokes. But in competition, the only thing that comes to mind is fear that they'll miss putts. They start trying to fix their strokes in the middle of the back nine. They finish the round trying something different on almost every putt.

I typically respond to calls from these clients by trying the equivalent of battlefield medicine. My first job is to stop the bleeding. I remind the player of how good he really is, regardless of what his mind is telling him at the moment. I remind him of how many of his peers and competitors would love to have the swing or the putting stroke that is giving him ulcers.

I might remind him that he's still got the skills to win. He just needs to stop letting his thinking prevent him from using them.

"You learned how to play great when you were still a kid and you've been in the top ten or top fifteen for years," I'll say. "So let's not pretend that you don't have the skills. You have the skills. You may have to keep your focus better on a few shots a day. You may have to change that focus a little so you're into the target. But you have the skills."

Maybe I talk about the way his mind worked when he was at the peak of his game. Players like these know what it is to think well. In their quest for improvement, or perfection, they've just stopped doing it.

I might remind a player that when he was on the top of his game, nothing mattered for him but his target. He was constantly in the present moment, thinking neither of the last swing nor the next one. All he cared about was the shot at hand and where he wanted it to send the ball. There was no such thing as a "next putt," as in "where do I want to leave this putt so my next putt will be easy?" Now he's constantly evaluating his last shot, critiquing its mechanics. He's thinking about the changes he'll make to his swing for the next tee shot before he hits the iron and the putts on the hole he's playing. Or he's chasing some mechanical notion that he thinks he must incorporate into his swing or his stroke.

If you think like that, you'll make yourself feel tight and awkward. You won't see the target, see the shot, and let it happen. You'll try to force it to happen.

If you were my client, I'd point out that we know that you can play the golf you need to win if you've got your mind where it needs to be. We have, as yet, no evidence you can play great golf when you're trying to force your body into certain positions.

"I want you into your target, to the exclusion of all else," I'd say. "I want you to have an indifferent attitude to whether the ball actually goes there. If you can do that, you'll be able to let it go. You can be indifferent on any given shot because you know that when you're in this zone where you're thinking about only the target, eventually you're going to score well. You're going to have peace of mind out there on the golf course."

This is, of course, a quick fix approach to the golfing mind. Quite often it helps, especially if it's a matter of getting the player back to employing mental skills and habits he's already learned and already believes in. I've had players shoot 76 in the first round of a tournament, alter their thinking after a long talk

Thursday night, and play their way back into the competition with a 66 on Friday.

It's not always that easy. Bad mental habits can be just as difficult to break as bad physical habits. The mind doesn't have switches. You can't turn good thinking on as easily as you can switch on an MP3 player.

I would much prefer that golfers never get into this position, whether they are pros or playing for pleasure. But most golfers do. It's the nature of the game and the nature of the people who tend to get good at it. They're strivers. They're used to working hard and seeing hard work pay off. They forget that in golf, you don't just have to work hard. You have to work smart. You can't ever forget that the mental game needs as much care and attention as the swing—perhaps more at the upper echelons of the game, where everyone has good swing mechanics. When you're trying to improve, you can't forget that when you're playing smart golf, it feels like you're not trying.

This book is designed to keep you playing smart golf. If you're trying to improve, and I assume you are, you're going to have to improve your thinking in tandem with your mechanics. Otherwise, the game will beat you up. You're going to have to make a commitment to mental discipline that you take as seriously as your commitment to a better swing.

4.

How Your Subconscious
Sees You

To develop the confidence that will see you through clutch golf situations, you must understand a few basic concepts about the human psyche. I say "concepts" rather than "facts" for a reason. We don't know the human psyche in the same way that we know, for instance, the internal combustion engine. We can't dismantle it, lay the parts on a lab bench, and put it back together. When I was teaching psychology at the University of Virginia, I used to begin courses by having my students read a book by a very skeptical scientist who examined all of the academic disciplines and poked holes in their assumptions. His basic conclusion about psychology was that we don't really know very much about the human mind, at least not in the sense that we know about geology.

So as I begin to talk about terms like the conscious mind, the subconscious mind, and the self-image, keep in mind that these are not tangible things like pistons, spark plugs, and carburetors. I know they exist within us. But ultimately, I know it as a matter of faith, just as I know that God exists. I have seen the evidence of God's presence in the world. I have seen the evidence of the conscious, the subconscious, and the self-image by the way they work in the minds of my clients.

Put simply, the conscious mind is that part of your mind that you're aware of. As you read this book, you're using your conscious mind. If you pause for a moment and consider what I'm saying, thinking about how it is reflected in you and your golf game, you're using your conscious mind. If you notice that your mouth feels a little dry and decide to put the book down and go get something to drink, you're using the conscious mind. If you go to the refrigerator, put your hands on a beer, and then put it back and drink water instead because you're watching your calories, that's a function of the conscious mind, too. The conscious mind is where your free will resides. It enables you to make choices about what you want for yourself and plan a way to achieve it. It enables you to take responsibility for yourself.

But it's your subconscious that rules your golf game. That's because golf is one of those physical activities, like driving a car, that are learned by the conscious brain and then controlled by the subconscious brain.

The subconscious brain is well suited to this assignment. If you're old enough to remember cars with manual transmissions, you already know this. When you were learning to drive, you used your conscious mind. You told yourself when and where to move the shift lever. You told yourself when and how to depress the clutch pedal. Your conscious mind was not an especially good driver. The car bucked, lurched, and stalled.

Eventually, though, you learned how to operate the car well enough so that control of your shifting switched to the subconscious mind. You stopped thinking about how to do it. You just did it, smoothly and effortlessly. With your subconscious mind in control of the transmission, your conscious mind was free to pick a radio station, have a conversation, or think about your golf game. You began to arrive at your destinations unaware of how many times you'd shifted gears or how you'd done it.

One major reason for that was the self-image you'd developed as a driver. During the learning phase of your driving career, your conscious mind evaluated how you were doing. You might have thought, "Hmm, that was a smooth shift. I'm getting the hang of this. In fact, I'm pretty good at it." Thoughts of that sort became the foundation for your self-image as a driver.

Self-image lives in the subconscious. We're not generally aware of it. Nor do we generally understand how influential self-image is.

We all have lots of self-images because we all play many roles in life. We have self-images as drivers, lovers, and, perhaps, parents. We have an image of ourselves in the working world. These self-images can vary dramatically. It's quite possible for someone to think of herself as a dynamic, capable lawyer but at the same time someone who's awkward and insecure in her personal relationships. It's quite possible for someone to feel like an instinctively capable and talented photographer but a clumsy golfer.

Self-image is not the same as self-esteem. I think of self-esteem as something we're all born with. It's connected with our basic dignity and worth as human beings. Without healthy self-esteem, it would be difficult, or impossible, to function.

Self-image is not inborn. We develop it for ourselves. It comes from many sources. The judgments of other people contribute to it. This is why I said Tiger Woods's parents did a great job of raising him. They evidently kept feeding him a steady diet of encouragement. Tiger listened, and their praise became part of his self-image. He arrived at adulthood feeling he was destined to do great things. That self-image was deeply rooted in his subconscious.

Obviously, it would be easier to have a strong, confident self-image if everyone around us was always telling us how good we are. Clients who complain to me about parents or coaches failing to provide that sort of encouragement have a point. But it's a limited point.

We are all the most important contributors to our own self-images. We do this in a number of ways. We process our own experiences. We judge them as successes or failures or something in between. That's called perception. We remember some experiences and we forget others. Does that three-footer you missed last weekend on the 17th hole of a crucial round keep popping back into your mind? Or do you remember all the putts of three feet and longer that you made and forget the one you missed? Or do you remember all of them? The way you process memories makes an enormous difference in your self-image.

In addition to perception and memory, we influence our self-image with our thinking and our imagination. The thoughts we have about ourselves as golfers affect our golfing self-image. So do the things we imagine ourselves doing.

You can think of the self-image as the sum of all the thoughts you've had about yourself. Some of them have been supplied by others. But most of them originate with you. These thoughts stay in the conscious brain for a while. They are then absorbed by the subconscious.

At any given moment, your self-image is like a register, stored in the subconscious, of all of this input. In some respects it might resemble a printout of all the input that a computer has ever received—data, commands, etc.

The subconscious is not particularly sophisticated. It doesn't evaluate this input to decide which data are valid and which are not. In that sense, it's like an income tax program. The program is going to take the numbers you feed it. It's not going to know whether those numbers are accurate. When it has all the input, it will spit out a number that represents what it thinks you owe the government. This computer program never errs. It always gives you the exact amount you owe—assuming that the numbers you fed it were correct. Of course, if someone were to give the program less than his full income, the computer would tell him he owed less to the government than he really did, a discrepancy that could be annoying in an audit.

Similarly, your subconscious self-image is not necessarily a very accurate or sophisticated reflection of yourself. It probably isn't identical to the considered judgment you would make about yourself. If, for instance, we met and talked about your golf game, you might in all sincerity tell me that, "I'm a pretty good golfer. I have some flaws in my game, like everyone else. But I hit it straight and I'm a good putter. My handicap comes down a stroke or so every season, and I think I can keep getting better. I like to compete and win." That would be your conscious mind's evaluation of yourself.

But you could simultaneously have a subconscious self-image that says, "I'm a choking dog." This would not be a particularly accurate self-image. It would be more akin to the self-image of the anorexia victim who looks at her spindly body in a mirror and thinks, "I'm fat." It would probably be based on a store of thoughts, memories, and other inputs that was skewed to the negative. Your subconscious self-image is based on the data you feed it, not necessarily on reality.

What you must understand is that in clutch situations, it's not your considered, conscious judgment of yourself as a golfer that dictates your performance. It's your subconscious self-image.

The subconscious will try to give you what it thinks you want. If you've developed a subconscious self-image as a golfer who chokes in the clutch, your subconscious will do what it can to make you choke in the clutch. It's very effective at doing this. On the other hand, if your subconscious self-image shows a player who wins championships, your subconscious will try to help you do that. And, again, it will be very effective at it.

That's all that confidence is, basically. It's a subconscious self-image of calm capability.

More than a century ago, the pioneering genius of American psychology, William James, wrote that, by and large, people tend to become what they think of themselves. The workings of the subconscious self-image demonstrate James's wisdom. There were no golf courses in the Massachusetts of the 19th century, where he formulated his theories. But if there had been, I suspect he would not have been in the least surprised at the way the mind influences golfing performance.

I see evidence of the influence of subconscious self-image in all the golfers I counsel. In many of them, the subconscious influences their scores almost as predictably as a thermostat regulates the temperature in a house. A professional may, for instance, have a self-image as a player who reliably shoots between 68 and 74. As long as he's within a few stokes of par, he's in his comfort zone. He plays his normal game. But if he makes a couple of double bogeys early in a round, he's suddenly in conflict with his subconscious self-image. More often than not, he'll make a few birdies to get himself back within his comfort zone, just as your air-conditioning will kick in if the temperature in your house rises more than a few degrees over your thermostat setting. Conversely, if the player birdies the first few holes, he's pushing against the lower edge of his comfort zone. I've had clients who tell me that it seems like every time they get a hot round going, they find themselves somehow making a couple of bogeys to cool themselves off. They're unaware that they have a comfort zone that mitigates against going low.

No ambitious professional golfer consciously wants to have this problem. The 65s and 66s are the rounds that earn big checks and win tournaments. But even after I've explained how the subconscious self-image works, I find that some of these clients resist making the changes they need to make.

Reconstructing your subconscious self-image can be an uncomfortable process. Suppose, for instance, that you see yourself as the sort of player who always makes a pretty good showing in the club championship but usually loses in the first couple of rounds to one of the truly "elite" players at the club. Or suppose you see yourself as the sort of player who gets and keeps her LPGA Tour card, maybe wins a lesser event every few years, makes a comfortable living, but never contends in majors or makes a Solheim Cup team. In either case, you'll probably perform at a level that comports with your subconscious self-image.

Changing your self-image can lead to some new kinds of distress. The club championship is no longer an occasion to have a couple of pleasant rounds, shake hands with the guy who beat you, and retreat to the bar for a friendly beer with your buddies. Just making a good living on the LPGA Tour is no longer going to satisfy you. You're going to have to contend with new expectations. You're suddenly going to be harshly disappointed if you lose in the second round of the club championship. Your comfortable spot in the middle tier of the LPGA Tour is no longer going to be comfortable. You're going to have to live up to all the potential within yourself, and potential can be a heavy burden.

So I sometimes have to challenge my clients. Do they dare to believe they can win? Do they dare to believe they can win a lot? Do they dare to put in the kind of work, both psychological and physical, that winning a lot would require? Do they dare to put themselves in the final group at a major on Sunday and let the world see how well they can handle the pressure? Do they dare risk feeling the hurt and disappointment if they fail? I tell them that I'm not asking them to dare to be the pope or the president or something really important. I'm just asking them to dare to be great at a game, to dare to win a silly golf tournament.

If the answer is yes, we're ready to begin the work of becoming a confident golfer. I'm going to teach you the mental regimen that will do it for you.

5.

Real Realism

Around this point in the proceedings, some clients furrow their brows and say, "Wait a minute, Doc! You're telling me that my own thoughts determine whether I'm confident or not, and that I need a better self-image. But I'm a realist. My self-image is based on the facts. I haven't won, so how can I be confident I can win? I know how I can play, and I know other guys can play better. So wouldn't I be fooling myself to think I can beat them?"

I can understand this. At first glance, it does seem that developing a winner's confidence before you actually win is reversing the natural order of things. But if you think about it, everyone has to win the first time. Once in a while, you see a tournament where everyone in contention falls apart and the winner is the last man standing. He may not have needed to feel confident he could win. It just happened to him. But that's relatively rare. Far more often, you see something like Zach Johnson going out and winning the 2007 Masters. Johnson had never won a major championship. He had Tiger Woods in pursuit and Tiger certainly didn't fall apart. Yet Johnson played confidently down the stretch and won.

We can do what Johnson did because we can control our own self-image. Every waking moment of every day, our conscious brain is processing thoughts, calling up memories, and choosing perceptions. Most of the time, we don't analyze or evaluate this mental activity. We just do it.

It's as if you were writing an essay, but you weren't keeping track of how many times you used passive verbs and active verbs, how crisp your sentences were, whether you had a logical paragraph structure, and so on. But, obviously, if you chose to, you could monitor and analyze your writing as you did it. You could remind yourself to prefer active verbs to passive verbs, to keep your sentences short, and to make sure each paragraph began with a clear topic sentence. You could spot each deviation from those rules as it occurred, hit the backspace key on your word processor, and change it.

The first step in changing your golfing self-image is monitoring your thoughts about your golf game. You need to become aware of exactly what comes into your mind. When you think back on your last round or your last tournament, what specifically do you think about? Do you think about the dozen drives you hit into the fairway or the two you hit into the woods? Do you think about the chips you left close to the hole or the one that you skulled over the green? Do you think about that fifteen-footer you sank or the four-footer you missed?

I ask these questions because one of the obstacles people often place in their own way is the notion that they're just being "honest" or "realistic" when they think about their golf games and dwell on their mistakes. Maybe this is because they had parents, teachers, or coaches who trained them to think that there was always room for improvement. I've known clients who actually won PGA Tour golf events but remembered and thought about only the bad shots they'd hit. They decided they were lucky, that the other players had fallen apart. They gave themselves no credit for winning. So their confidence did not improve as a result of their win.

I had a client who sank a chip or a pitch at least every other round he played, yet dwelt on a chip he hit fat and left off the green to cost his club a league title—ten years ago. When I asked this client to begin monitoring his thoughts about his golf game, he could see where I was going. He immediately became suspicious that I was going to trick him into some kind of fraudulent confidence, that I was going to ask him to think only of his good shots and in effect lie to himself.

I explained to him that he was the one lying to himself. But he was lying in a negative way. He was constantly dredging up the memory of one bad shot and doing his best to forget all the good ones he'd hit. Most of his chips and pitches were pretty good. But by focusing on that one big mistake, he had developed the self-image of someone who couldn't get the ball up and down in the clutch. His subconscious, being a simple, yet accommodating mechanism, tried to give him what it thought he wanted. It tried to make him panic and mishit clutch chips and pitches. This is simply the way the subconscious works. It's the basis for the phenomenon popularly known as the self-fulfilling prophecy. You instill in your subconscious the idea that something unfortunate is going to happen. And then, even though your conscious mind doesn't want this unfortunate outcome, your subconscious contrives to make the disaster happen.

Suppose, to use an example from another field, you were a teenager with a self-image as a klutz around girls. You were too shy to ask anyone out. You were afraid you'd embarrass yourself somehow if you did. Whenever you saw a girl you were attracted to, you'd think, "She couldn't ever see anything in me. She's out of my league."

Then one day, your sister comes to you and says her very attractive friend Cynthia thinks you're cute and wants to go out on a double date. You agree to go. But on the date, even though you want to impress Cynthia, you can't get around your subconscious self-image. The other three people carry on a conversation, but you're always thinking of something witty to say a few seconds after the subject has changed. You spill pizza on your white shirt. The evening progresses from gaffe to gaffe. When you finally drop Cynthia at her house, she gives you a quick, limp handshake and can't get through the door quickly enough.

You go home thinking, "Well, I was right. A girl like Cynthia could never be interested in me." But your sister asks, "What got into you? You weren't your normal self." You realize she's right. You weren't your normal self. You behaved like a klutz because that's what your subconscious thought you wanted.

My client who dwelt on his bad chips and pitches could accept the idea of the subconscious affecting his mind, but he found it hard to believe that the subconscious could have an involuntary effect on his body. Since golf is a physical activity, he found it hard to imagine the subconscious affecting his performance. So I asked him to close his eyes and imagine a certain scenario.

I asked him whether he had a favorite dish. He said shrimp jambalaya.

"What a coincidence," I said. "Emeril Lagasse is a friend of ours, and he's visiting tonight. You know he cooks the best shrimp jambalaya in the world."

"I've seen him on TV," my client said.

"Well, he's going to cook your favorite dish for our dinner. He's going to bring tomatoes and peppers and spices to steam with the rice. He's going to peel the shrimp, then blanch them. They're big and juicy and tender. He'll add a few special things, like a little andouille sausage. Then he'll put it all together and we'll sit in the kitchen and just savor the smell as it cooks."

My client smiled. It was late afternoon.

"I'm getting hungry," he said. "My stomach is growling."

"I'll bet your mouth is watering, too," I said.

He nodded.

"Well, there's one more thing I have to tell you," I said. "The shrimp is infected with salmonella. You're going to be as sick as a dog for three days after you eat it."

He opened his eyes and sat bolt upright.

"Your mouth still watering?" I asked him.

"No."

"Stomach still growling?"

"I've lost my appetite."

"And you still don't think the mind can affect the body?"

He shook his head.

In fact, the mind can cause involuntary effects on the body far more dramatic that a simple loss of appetite. If you find yourself in a situation where your conscious mind is attempting to overrule a strong impulse generated by a subconscious self-image, your body can react with a form of panic. You can feel shortness of breath, perspiration, and nausea.

This is why golfers who don't have a strong self-image yet find themselves in contention in a tournament sometimes report that they felt almost ill in the clutch. Their conscious mind was insisting that they stay calm, focused, and cool. Their subconscious urge was to play in a way that conformed to their self-image as chokers. Their bodies reacted to this conflict in much the same way that they would in an airplane that suddenly lost cabin pressure and dived.

I can't, of course, tell how your subconscious mind will affect your body on the golf course. I can't tell whether your subconscious self-image comports with either your conscious self-image or the reality of your golf game. You have to determine those things. All I can tell you for sure is that your subconscious will very definitely affect your motor skills on the golf course.

To find out whether it will help you or hurt you, the inevitable first step is monitoring your own thoughts. The best way to do this, I've found, is in writing. Get a little notebook and carry it around. Every time you have a thought or a recollection about your golf game, write it down. Once a day, if you like, transfer the notes to a computer file. In short order, you'll have begun to compile a facsimile of the input your conscious brain is giving to your subconscious brain every day. You'll begin to see what kind of self-image you create for yourself.

I understand that some golfers will resist this step. They'd be embarrassed to be seen, at lunch, for instance, whipping out a notebook and scribbling down a thought about their putting. They wouldn't want people asking them what they were doing. They wouldn't want anyone to know they were worried about their confidence. For others, the notion of writing down their thoughts just seems too introspective.

All right. You don't have to write them down. Writing them down makes it easier to remember your thoughts and to see the sum of the inputs you're giving to your subconscious self-image. But it's not imperative. You can opt to keep track of your thoughts on golf mentally. This will require more effort on your part, although it may not seem so at first. It may seem that writing things down is the real effort. But the effort of remembering the thoughts you notice and classifying them may, in the long run, be more cumbersome.

Either way you do it, the project should be very revealing.

You may realize that for years you've been dwelling on mistakes. You've implanted thousands of negative thoughts in your subconscious self-image. It's as if you've given yourself a heavy garbage bag to carry around every time you play golf—and you can't put it down when it's time to hit the ball.

This can be a daunting realization. If you've been accumulating negative ideas in your subconscious for years, you might assume that you're stuck with a subconscious self-image as a choker. Or you might assume it will take just as long to counterbalance that negative data with the sort of positive thoughts that create a confident self-image.

Fortunately, you would be wrong.

The happy fact is that as your subconscious constantly

updates your self-image, some data weigh more heavily than others. Recent thoughts you have had about yourself are going to be much more significant than things you thought about yourself a year ago, to say nothing of ten years ago. This works two ways, of course. If you used to be confident, but you've been thinking negatively recently, those negative thoughts will quickly erode your subconscious self-image. But if you get back on track, you can repair the damage fairly quickly.

Not only do recent thoughts weigh more heavily than old ones, the most influential thoughts are the ones you associate with strong emotions. That's because they stick in the memory far longer, and they rise to the level of conscious thought more often. You probably remember your first romantic kiss, even if it happened many years ago and you have long since lost track of the person you kissed. You may not remember anything about the good-bye kiss you exchanged with your spouse a week ago Tuesday. It's not because you don't love your spouse. But good-bye kisses can get to be routine, and we rarely get emotional about routine events. On the other hand, just before that first romantic kiss, you may have been trembling with nervous anticipation, with a heady mix of joy, fear, and love. So the kiss cemented itself in your memory. If it was successful—by which I mean you both smiled and your braces didn't lock together—it probably helped you develop a subconscious self-image as a person reasonably attractive to the opposite sex.

This leads to two conclusions. One is that you can develop a confident subconscious self-image if you begin to monitor your thoughts and make a successful effort to feed your subconscious the kind of data that build confidence. The other is that you can accelerate the process if you can learn to attach strong emotions to positive, encouraging thoughts and memories and little or no emotion to the negative.

You may think that your thoughts and emotions are involuntary, that you can't control them. I'm going to tell you how you can.

6.

Remember to Remember

I have a client, Mark Wilson, who's about the same age as Tiger Woods. But that was all their golfing resumes had in common until recently. Tiger was a success as soon as he turned pro. Mark was one of those players who struggle to stay on the PGA Tour. He grew up in Wisconsin, where the golf season is short, and while Tiger was winning junior events worldwide, Mark's claim to fame was a Wisconsin high school championship. He finished at the University of North Carolina in 1997, turned pro, and spent six years grinding on golf's minor league level, playing before nonexistent crowds, doubling up in cheap motel rooms, knowing that only a very high finish would earn back a tournament's entry fee. (It's one of the ironies of professional golf that the millionaires on PGA Tour pay a $100 entry fee for each tournament, a figure that hasn't changed in years. The struggling novices on the mini-tours pay tournament entry fees two and three times that high.) He got to the PGA Tour in 2003, but he never quite managed to earn enough money to keep his playing privileges for the next season. Mark compiled the dubious distinction of playing in the tour's qualifying tournament ten times.

He first came to see me in the fall of 2006, as he was preparing for his tenth trip to Q-school. From that fact alone, I knew he was a determined guy. I knew he wasn't a quitter. And I admire those qualities.

But one of the toughest challenges a player in Mark's situation faces is maintaining his confidence. As years go by and the goal of success on the PGA Tour remains just out of reach, it can be tough for a player to continue to see himself as a winner. It can be easy to start dwelling on missed shots and missed opportunities. It can be easy to feed the subconscious the sort of thoughts that undermine confidence instead of building it up. This is why players don't progress at a steady rate as they play and gain experience. They may be learning better ways to hit the ball; they may be learning better ways to manage their games in tournament situations; they may be learning how to handle life on the road. But if they're not becoming more confident as they learn these things, it can be all for naught.

Mark had played more than 100 events on the PGA Tour, but he would have been the first to tell you he didn't believe he could win there. I suggested that he improve his subconscious self-image by keeping a journal. I wanted it to be a special kind of journal.

In it, I wanted Mark to record every good shot he hit every day. I didn't care if it was just a 5-iron he pured on the practice range warming up. I wanted him to write it down. Mark agreed. Every night he wrote down or typed into a computer file all of his good shots. He then read and reread the list.

Keeping the journal accomplished several things for Mark. Obviously, it required him to recall all of his good shots. He had to remember them in detail in order to write them down and describe them. So each night, he was reliving the good shots that he'd made. The act of writing reinforced the memory of those good shots. Over time, Mark began to enjoy the process of writing in his journal. He liked pulling out the handwritten version and reading it at various times during his day. The process helped him learn to take pleasure in his good shots. And, as time went on, he realized that the vast majority of his shots every day were good ones. He hit more good shots than he had time to write down.

Equally important was what the journal prevented him from doing. He no longer went back to his room and brooded over his bad shots.

By staying with this process, Mark dramatically improved the input he was giving his subconscious. He quickly saw results. Five months after we started working together, Mark was playing in the Honda Classic down in Florida. His tournament chances diminished on Friday at the 5th hole. There was a backup there, and the group behind Mark was waiting on the tee by the time he hit his shot. One of the players peered into Mark's bag to see what club was missing. This is legal; there's nothing in the rules that says a player can't look into another player's bag. But the conversation that ensued veered into illegality.

"What club did he use?" the waiting player asked his own caddie.

"Some kind of hybrid," the caddie answered.

Mark's caddie heard this exchange and without thinking about it, volunteered some information. "It's an 18-degree," he said.

That, unfortunately, violated the rule against giving advice to another competitor. Mark's caddie realized it right away and told Mark. Mark notified a rules official and was assessed a two-stroke penalty.

But in this tournament, Mark did not let the incident shake the confidence he'd been developing. Despite spotting two strokes to the field, he shot a 66 that day, with four birdies on the back nine. And he was in contention in the final round, along with Boo Weekly, Camilo Villegas, and José Coceres. In the clutch, he showed confidence commensurate with his integrity. He rolled in a forty-seven-footer to save par on the 70th hole. He made it into the playoff with an eight-footer on the final hole. He sank a thirty-footer to stay alive on the first playoff hole, then made a ten-foot birdie putt to win on the third playoff hole.

That's clutch performance. That's what Mark's improved confidence allowed him to do. He had never won before. Those who think that confidence can grow only from winning would have predicted he'd melt down in the crucible of pressure he faced in the final holes. They would have been wrong. Confidence doesn't depend on experience. It depends on how you choose to think.

I've had other clients who benefited from keeping journals. One of them, Nicole Hage, was a four-time all-American at Auburn University. She liked the process of writing in her journal so much that she started writing about her good shots as she played. She'd hit one and then, as she walked toward the ball for her next shot, she'd pull out her notebook and jot down her thoughts. She found that it helped her stay calm and positive during that long period between shots when a golfer most needs to keep her mind focused on the right things.

Skeptics may read about this and think that I'm saying that a golfer who keeps a journal of his or her good shots will become an immediate winner. I'm not saying that. I understand that golf is a game of both confidence and competence. If you haven't mastered the fundamental shots, you're not going to win any tournaments (unless you're getting handicap strokes). You need to make sure that your physical skills match your aspirations. What is important is that you improve both mentally and physically. Mark and Nicole have the physical skills. They needed more confidence, and they got it by using journals to change the nature of the data they were feeding their subconscious minds.

If your physical skills are adequate only to break 100, you won't start shooting in the 70s just by developing confidence. But if you develop confidence, you'll be shooting in the 90s, even when you play your buddies for that hotly contested $2 Nassau.

Some clients will listen to all this and ask, "What do I do about the bad shots I hit that day? Do you want me just to forget them?"

Well, yes.

There are certain things a golfer can learn from a bad performance, and I'll discuss them later on. But for the most part, the smart thing to do about bad shots is forget them.

You'll be helped in this if you can train yourself to do two things. One is to assign the same relatively low level of importance to every shot, no matter what the circumstances. You need to care enough about a shot to keep yourself from getting sloppy with your setup and your execution. But you can't care too much about the results. If you must be intense, be intense about the preparatory part of the shot rather than the result. Be intense about whether you had your mind where it needed to be, about whether you committed yourself to your plan, about whether you got into your target, about whether you followed your routine. Don't be intense about where the ball actually went. If you refuse to assign a high level of emotion to the results of a shot, it will make it very much easier to forget the bad ones.

Conversely, after you've hit a good shot, don't treat it as a normal, expectable event. A good golf shot is a small miracle. If you don't believe that, watch some beginners trying simply to hit the ball. Golf is hard, and when you pull off a shot, you've managed to coordinate your body and your mind at a high level of skill. Rejoice in that. You can be quiet about it or you can show your pleasure. That's a matter of personal style. But be the opposite of the guy who shrugs phlegmatically when he hits a great shot and loses his temper when he hits a poor one. That guy is working to make his memory a handicap rather than an aid. He's probably going to remember his bad shots and forget his good ones.

I know that even though this focus on remembering and dwelling on good shots works, it goes against some people's grain. They refuse to do it. For them, I have one suggestion. If they're not going to figure out ways to feed positive, confidence-building ideas to their subconscious, they ought to try not to think about golf at all when they're away from the course. Think about the stock market or about the good novel you're reading. Give golf a rest.

7.

Mental Gymnastics

I've alluded to the idea that improving your confidence is not an instantaneous event. There are no lightning bolts of inspiration, no lightbulbs clicking on. The subconscious self-image is very malleable, but it doesn't change overnight. It changes because of the accretion of thoughts over time. If you want to be a confident golfer, you have to think the way great golfers do. If your particular issue is putting or chipping or driving, you will need to think the way great putters, chippers, and drivers do. There's no way I can tell you exactly how long this period of remolding the subconscious self-image will take in your particular case. It depends on what your self-image was like when you began trying to change it and on how seriously and effectively you commit to the process.

In that sense, developing confidence is very much like improving your fitness. How long an individual needs to get fit depends on where he starts and what he does every day to improve. In a fitness program, there would probably be more concentrated work to do at the beginning. Maybe you'd need to go on a diet to lose some weight. You'd have to work out every day to strengthen and tone muscles that had atrophied from disuse. Eventually, if you stuck with it, you'd reach your goals for weight, strength, and so on. But, as I said earlier, you would not forever own that level of fitness once you got it. You'd have to work to maintain it. You might not have to be quite so strict with your calorie intake, but you would still have to watch what you ate and get on the scale every morning. You might not have to work out every day, but you'd have to work out several times a week to keep those muscles toned.

In much the same way, your confidence needs a regimen.

By regimen, I don't mean simply thinking about your golf game. I know players who hurt their confidence by thinking about their golf game. They're constantly calling to mind bad shots. Their minds operate the way television crews sometimes do when they cover a football game where someone gets injured. They play and replay the footage of the injury, at every speed, from every angle. These golfers replay their bad shots over and over again. As far as confidence is concerned, that's like trying to lose weight by eating a couple of slices of chocolate cake every evening. It's not going to work.

You've already seen one valuable component of a mental regimen that builds confidence. It's the journal where you record all of your good shots. But what about days when you don't play golf? What can you do then?

You can write affirmations. An affirmation is a simple, positive thought about your golf game. The more specific an affirmation is, the better. It's better to write, "Under pressure, I have a smooth putting stroke," than it is to write, "I am a good golfer."

Make your affirmations positive. It's better to write, "I am comfortable when I'm in a position to win," than it is to write, "I am no longer uncomfortable when I'm in a position to win."

Write your affirmations in the present tense. Telling yourself, "I stick with my routine in every situation" is more powerful than saying, "I will stick with my routine in every situation."

In the first appendix at the back of this book, I've written some sample affirmations for you. But they're only samples. I want you to write your own. You wouldn't play your best golf swinging my clubs or wearing my shoes. You won't develop confidence as well as you could if you use my affirmations.

I've had clients who instinctively shy away from the act of writing affirmations. Maybe they don't like to write. Maybe the act of writing affirmations seems too much like an admission that they have mental flaws. Maybe they're afraid someone will see it and laugh at them. This makes little sense to me. You can go to any practice green at a PGA Tour event and see any number of training aids that players are using. It might be a block of wood with a curved edge that is supposed to train the putter head to open, come back to square, and close during the stroke. It might be a putter with a small metal sphere where the blade should be that is supposed to train the player to make contact precisely in the sweet spot of the putter; otherwise the ball will glance off to one side or the other. And, as you know if you watch golf on television, there is no end to devices that promise to cure the flaws in the full swing. Very few players I know would be embarrassed to be seen on the practice range swinging a club with a hinge in the shaft in hopes that it will give them a better, smoother backswing. But, some of these same players would be embarrassed to have a list of their affirmations posted on the locker room bulletin board. So they don't write them.

If that sounds like you, I can only advise you to find some

way to get the right kinds of thoughts flowing through your conscious mind and into your subconscious every day. Recognizing your strengths should in no way embarrass you. Writing affirmations ought to be an occasion of quiet pride.

But great coaches have always understood that not all athletes will do this. That's why their locker rooms are full of affirmations. John Wooden's UCLA basketball teams saw his "Pyramid of Success" every day as they prepared for practice. Among other things, that reminded them of Coach Wooden's belief that, "The strongest steel is well-founded self-belief. It is earned, not given."

I don't put myself in John Wooden's class as a sports psychologist. But it might be, as it was with the UCLA basketball teams he coached, that reading someone else's affirmations can help you, even though I don't believe that it will help you as much as writing your own. I know, for instance, that Dana Quigley has taped "Rotella's Rules," which were printed in *Golf Is Not a Game of Perfect*, to his golf cart. Dana is a shining example of someone who developed confidence despite a history of early failure. He wasn't a great junior player, he couldn't stick on the PGA Tour, and he doesn't have a classic swing. But when he got his chance to play the Champions Tour, he seized it. He did the things he needed to do to see himself as a winner. One of those things was giving his mind the kind of input it needed.

Be detailed. You might, for instance, write something like:

"I am a great pitcher of the golf ball. When I pitch the ball, it feels so beautiful. I love my rhythm. I love my flow. I just see the shot I want to hit and do it. I love the solid way the ball comes off the club. I love the way it sounds. I can feel the clubhead contact the ball, then the ground. I love watching the ball hit the green, bite, and roll to the hole."

You might have different affirmations for each department of your golf game. The ones you emphasize will depend on your particular strengths and weaknesses.

Neither your affirmations nor mine will work, however, if you treat them as wallpaper. You have to read them carefully and think about them. You have to buy into them.

If you're the sort who'd be embarrassed if someone read your affirmations, I'd suggest that you stop paying so much attention to what other people think. The golf world is full of commentators. They exist at the professional level. They exist at your local course. They are generally very good at reaching the conclusion that what has worked is brilliant and what hasn't worked is not. Sometimes they're right, and sometimes they're not. Suppose Zach Johnson had been overtaken by Tiger Woods in the last round of the 2007 Masters. The newspapers would have been full of commentaries to the effect that a short hitter with a conservative strategy, like Johnson, couldn't win at Augusta. As it turned out, Tiger didn't catch Johnson in the last few holes. So all the commentators said that Johnson's win proved that a short hitter with a conservative strategy could win at Augusta.

The point is that outside commentators are the last thing Zach Johnson, or anyone else, should believe in.

Believe in yourself. Believe in your own internal commentator. Make sure that your commentator is telling you things that will help you. Write affirmations.

8.

The Problem with Perfection

If you take my advice and commit yourself to a program that will improve your confidence by changing your subconscious self-image, you will in all likelihood improve. But as you improve, you'll encounter new challenges. One of them is the problem of perfection.

I know it sounds paradoxical. Isn't perfection the absence of problems? Yes, it is. But the truth is that perfection doesn't exist in golf and never will. It can become a problem if golfers either choose to pursue it or ascribe it to someone else.

Competitive golfers tend to be ambitious, driven people. They have high expectations for themselves. They set goals and work to achieve them. All of that is good.

But when an ambitious, driven golfer falls prey to perfectionism, he is at risk in many ways.

First, he's never going to be satisfied. As soon as even one thing goes wrong, he's always going to be telling himself (and his subconscious) that he's failed. This can put more than his golfing confidence in jeopardy. It can also lead to depression and burnout. I've seen many talented athletes become perfectionists and ultimately quit their sports rather than suffer through the pain that accompanies perfectionism.

Don't measure yourself against an impossible standard of perfection. Perfect golf swings and perfect golf shots are extremely rare. A truly confident golfer doesn't care how often he achieves either of these things, and he certainly doesn't let his confidence be affected by something as mythical as perfection. He knows that he can't expect perfection in his mental game any more than he can in his physical game.

I've had clients who get started on a program to improve their confidence and then sadly admit to me that they're still having the occasional negative thought about their games, and they're afraid those thoughts are spoiling their subconscious self-image.

I try to get players like that to relax. No one's thoughts are purely positive. If you can push the ratio of positive thoughts to 90 or 95 percent, you're doing better than nearly all of your competition. You're doing more than well enough.

The golfer with real, durable, and useful confidence believes not in perfection, whether mental or physical, but in his ability to score. If he's playing tournament golf, he believes he can get the ball in the hole more efficiently than anyone else in the field. He's not interested in whether he does this by hitting fairways and greens with perfect regularity. If he has to scramble for his pars and birdies, that's fine with him. He knows that once a tournament is over, no one cares who hit the most greens in regulation. They remember only who won.

Many golfers have a slightly different problem with perfectionism. They think someone else is perfect, or at least much closer to it than they are. Maybe you're playing in a club event and you come up against the scratch player who's won the event five times running. Or maybe it's just Joe, the guy in your regular foursome whose handicap is always a stroke or two better than yours and who always seems to find his way into your wallet. You may realize Joe is less than a perfect golfer, but he seems to have a perfect record against you. Maybe you play for a small, lightly regarded college golf program and you come up against an all-American with a suitcase full of press clippings. Or maybe you're a professional who gets into the final pairing of a tournament for the first time—and hello, Tiger Woods.

Whether it's Joe or Tiger, a golfer has got to get over the notion that anyone he faces is perfect. If you give the idea a moment's thought, its absurdity becomes evident.

Take Tiger. He's a great scorer, yes. But he's hardly perfect. He sometimes doesn't know where his driver is going; he has to leave it in the bag. He sometimes has trouble controlling the length of his irons. His putting can be ordinary.

Yet many commentators, journalists, and fellow competitors have trouble acknowledging to themselves that Tiger is flawed. They rave about the 2-iron stinger he hits but overlook the fact that he hits it when he can't be sure he'll find the fairway with his driver. They marvel at his recovery shots, like the one he chipped into the 16th hole at Augusta at the 2004 Masters, but they ignore the fact that he hit his tee shot over the green. When Tiger bumps a ball with a fairway wood from the fringe of the green, they applaud his imagination rather than consider the possibility that he's nervous about chipping from a tight, downhill lie. When Tiger goes hole after hole without making a putt, they attribute it to remarkably tricky greens, as at Oakmont in 2007, rather than consider the possibility that Tiger was mortal enough to get a little tentative and defensive.

Don't misunderstand me. I am not saying that Tiger is not a marvelous player. He is. I am only saying he isn't perfect. He can be beaten.

But he won't be beaten, at least not very often, by people who think he's perfect.

If you think you're playing against someone who's perfect, two things tend to happen. One is that you decide you can win only if you're also perfect. So you try to force yourself to hit perfect shots. You tighten up. You try too hard. Instead of getting better, your shotmaking gets worse. When that happens, you get discouraged, because you've already convinced yourself that only perfection will be good enough. So you play less than your best golf, and your "perfect" opponent needs to play only decently to win.

Rather than being a perfectionist, you would be much better off adopting the perspective of Joe, the guy who's taking your money every Saturday. Joe knows he isn't perfect, but he also knows that against you he doesn't have to be. He can beat you by playing his normal game and waiting for things to happen. In that frame of mind, Joe doesn't get too concerned if you go up a hole or two in the early going. He stays relaxed and confident. When he's relaxed and confident, Joe plays his best. Maybe he chips in for birdie on a hole you thought he'd bogey. Maybe when he gets the honor, he hits an iron to within tap-in range on a par three.

Partly because you are hypersensitive to his calm demeanor,

you don't let yourself relax. Because you don't see yourself as a guy who can beat Joe, playing well doesn't seem to help you. If you go up two in the first few holes, your subconscious will panic. It thinks you don't want to beat Joe, and it tries to give you what you want. So you miss fairways and greens you would normally hit. You lose your rhythm. Your chipping and putting get tentative. You struggle with yourself, thinking, "Why can't I just hit the ball the way I know I can hit it?" When the match is over, you manage to shake hands with Joe, but you walk off the golf course irritated and frustrated. You think that you've choked or that Joe has some sort of hex on you.

You have to understand that no golfer is perfect. And you have to love your own ability more than the ability of anyone you face. If you don't, you might consider a hiatus from serious competition. Work on your confidence and work on your game until you feel you can beat anyone you face, whether it be Tiger Woods or the guys you go to Florida with every winter.

Here's an activity you can try. Go to a golf tournament. It doesn't have to be a PGA Tour or an LPGA event. It can be a collegiate championship or a mini-tour event. Just make it one in which the players are ones you consider clearly superior to yourself. Walk with the best player in the event. Chart his or her round. Record how often he hits the fairway off the tee, how often she hits a green in regulation. Make a note of every shot that is less than perfect. You're going to find, of course, that even the straightest hitters miss a fifth of the fairways and a quarter of the greens. They're not perfect. The act of charting this imperfection will help you realize how irrelevant perfection is to your own golf game and your aspirations to improve it.

If you walk onto the course loving your own ability and knowing that no one is perfect, you won't automatically and always win, of course. But you're far more likely to walk off the course feeling, "I liked the way I played today. I enjoyed that."

Finding that feeling is one of the best reasons to play golf.

9.

What You See Is What You Get

One of the best things about a regimen to build confidence is that you can do part of it in bed. Not that you have to. You can do it anywhere. I'm talking about the process of visualization. I'm talking about the vivid imagination of things you want to happen. It's a sort of mental rehearsal that can help turn dreams into reality. It's a key component of your effort to build and sustain the confidence you'll need in clutch situations.

Jack Nicklaus used to talk about watching movies in his mind; it was part of his preshot routine. The notion of going to the movies is a useful one, one that applies to both your preshot routine and your off-course efforts to develop a winner's confidence. Your subconscious brain doesn't understand the difference between imagination and reality the way your conscious brain does. If you do it right, visualizing what you want to happen tells your subconscious that the shot you're about to hit is nothing you can't handle. To your subconscious, you've already proven you can do it.

To some golfers, this idea seems just as alien as writing affirmations. But I've found that players who spurn visualization tend to be people who are already doing a lot of it. The problem is that they're either imagining or remembering all the worst things that can happen to them on a golf course. They replay their bad shots, sometimes bad shots from years ago. They recollect them in vivid detail. Or they anticipate mistakes they're afraid they're going to make the following day in the big match against a rival school.

The subconscious treats all of this recollected and imagined material as fodder for your self-image. It perceives these images as things you want to happen again. When the time comes, it tries to give you what it thinks you want.

Remember that the subconscious self-image is very impressionable. You can practice for hours at a time, until you're striking the ball, or chipping it, or putting it just the way you want to. The memory of those good practice shots helps to form your subconscious self-image. It will help even more if you keep a journal and list the good shots you've made, reinforcing the memory and the subconscious input. But if you then leave the range or the practice green or your writing desk and start envisioning bad shots, you can undo all the psychological benefits of a good practice session.

That's one of the reasons I urge clients to make visualization a part of their daily mental regimen. Visualize yourself hitting both your favorite shots and shots that you haven't actually made yet. Visualizing yourself hitting a soft, delicate pitch off a tight lie to a pin tucked just behind a bunker can be almost as beneficial as hitting that shot in practice. It can even do something more—it can simulate the pressure of hitting that delicate pitch in a clutch situation. That can make it easier for you when the need for that pitch arises in a tournament.

The psychology of visualization stems from the psychology

of dreams. You may have experienced, for example, a vivid nightmare. Your dream was very detailed. Its frightening aspects seemed, to your sleeping mind, all too real. When you woke up, you experienced some of the physical symptoms of an actual fright experience. Your heart was racing. You might have been panting or sweating. All of that happened because your subconscious system can't distinguish between a real event and a vividly imagined event. It can, however, distinguish between a real event and a casual thought. You can't be halfhearted about visualization if you want it to work.

In order to visualize effectively, you need to devote the same sort of attention and effort that you'd expect to apply to physical practice. You don't see players who are working seriously on their putting strokes handling the club with one hand while the other props a phone against their ears so they can chat with their brokers. If they're doing that, they're not improving their putting strokes. Good players have a knack for going into a little bubble when they practice. They block out all distractions. They focus intently on what they're doing. If they have an instructor with them, they listen intently to him and only him. When you visualize, you need to be just as intently focused.

Don't be deceived when you see players chatting with agents, equipment company representatives, fellow players, or even gallery members on the range at a PGA Tour event. Some of the great players have been great gabbers; Lee Trevino, memorably, was one of them. But when a player is hitting shots on the range at a tournament and talking at the same time, he's only trying to loosen up. When he really wants to work on something, he quiets down and concentrates. And for every minute he spends chatting on a tournament practice tee, you can bet he's spent a silent hour alone on a range somewhere, doing his real preparation. Good practice, whether mental or physical, takes intensity.

So if you're going to visualize, you need to turn off the television, turn off the phone, and turn off the computer. You may want to turn off the lights. You'd better not try to do it while you're driving your car.

The best location for visualization varies. Touring pros, obviously, spend a lot of time in hotel rooms, and a hotel room can be an ideal place for visualizing. They also spend a lot of time on airplanes. If you can develop the knack of shutting everything else out during a flight, closing your eyes, and visualizing, so much the better. You can make productive use of time that otherwise might be wasted. But anyplace where you can shut out distractions will do. Moviemakers know that their films work best on audiences when the audience is in a theater rather than, say, an airport waiting area. In the theater, it's dark and it's quiet. In those conditions, it's easiest to get wrapped up in the sounds and images of the film. You want to try to create the same sort of conditions for the film you're going to create in your mind.

Once you've decided where you're going to do your visualization, focus in detail on how and what you will visualize. Detail is extraordinarily important. Again, think of yourself as a creative artist. A good writer or filmmaker will put a lot of effort into the details that establish setting. They'll tell you, or show you, a thousand things about the scene. They want the reader or the viewer to know how hot or how cold it is, what color the curtains in a window are, and exactly how the light glints off a woman's hair. Think of J. K. Rowling and her enormously successful Harry Potter books. One of the reasons they work so well is her careful attention to all of the intriguing details about Harry's magical world. Vivid details suck the viewer into the film or book experience and make it seem more real.

So, if you're visualizing a golf shot, pay the same sort of attention to detail. Use all of your senses. Is it hot and humid? Feel the sweat beading on your forehead and your damp shirt sticking to your shoulders. Is it windy? Hear the way the breeze sounds in your ears when you turn your face toward it. Watch the leaves in the trees downwind turn from green to grayish as the wind forces their undersides up. See a few blades of grass swirl away as you toss them into a gust. Is the sun out? See the shadows you cast on the green. Smell the new-mown fairways and the flowers that grow by the clubhouse. If you're a tournament player, you'll want to see the scoreboards and the galleries and the photographers crouching inside the ropes. All of these details will make the imagined experience seem that much more real and convincing to you.

Change the details. You'll want to prepare, for instance, for any wind and weather conditions. Imagine yourself playing in the rain, meticulously keeping your grips and gloves dry, taking pride in your ability to stay calm and focused in the face of adverse conditions. Imagine yourself feeling a stiff wind in your face as you step onto the tee. Imagine how you'll handle it. Imagine a moving photographer distracting you as you start to swing. Imagine yourself calmly stopping, waiting for stillness, and then restarting your preshot routine.

You'll want to imagine being nervous. Feel the sweat on

your palms, if that's what nerves do to you. Feel the churning in your gut. Feel the way your conscious mind struggles in a tight spot to stay positive—and succeeds.

There are two basic points of view for this sort of exercise. Some people imagine as if they were a camera filming themselves. It's an out-of-body look at yourself in action. More commonly, people imagine the experience as if they were living it. They see what their eyes would see, hear what their ears would hear, and so on. I prefer this second approach. I think it's more intimate, more vivid, and therefore more effective. But there are virtues to the first approach as well. One is that you can see your whole body executing a shot. You may want to experiment and see which point of view seems more helpful to you. You may want to try both at different times.

Whichever point of view you choose, you want to see yourself successfully executing your shots. You want to see the ball going where you want it to go, with the trajectory you want to give it. You want to see the ball going in the hole. You want to feel the emotional satisfaction of a shot that comes off exactly as you planned it. You want to hear the applause, if applause is what you can expect when you win.

You'll want to envision different scenarios. When I was on the staff at the University of Virginia, I used to lead the basketball team through its pregame mental preparation. I'd tell them to imagine themselves leading all the way. Then I'd turn it around and talk them through a scenario in which they fell behind early and had to come back.

You can do much the same thing in visualizing a round of golf. What will it be like if you start off hot and play the last six holes with a lead? What if it's just the first round and you get off to a good start? Can you envision yourself continuing to be hot and shooting a truly low score? Conversely, what will it be like if you start poorly? Can you envision yourself sticking with your game plan and recovering? Can you envision yourself staying calm and coming from behind to win?

Envision the people you're going to be playing with. Imagine them being chatty and distracting. Imagine them being cold and aloof. Imagine them taking so much time to look for a lost ball that you start to worry about time. Imagine them making birdies and challenging you to match them.

By all means, if you're preparing for a tournament, imagine the course you'll be playing. See if you can visualize an entire round on it. Begin on the first hole. You're up. You aim down the right side of the fairway. Your preshot routine helps you overcome the usual starting jitters. You feel your body coil. You see your left shoulder come under your eyes. You feel smooth and relaxed, yet powerful. Your timing is in synch. Your balance is instinctive. You hear the solid click as clubhead meets ball. The feeling transmitted from the clubhead to your hands tells you that you got it right in the sweet spot. You finish with your weight well balanced over your left leg, the toes of your right foot bearing almost no weight at all. You're so steady that you could hold that pose for hours. You watch your ball start just inside the tree line, then draw gently into the fairway. You reach down to pick up your tee. You walk down the path cut through the rough, connecting the tee to the fairway. Birds chirp in the trees, matching your mood. It's always good to hit that first one well. You feel calm, vibrant, confident.

You repeat this process for every shot you're going to play, or until you fall asleep.

You visualize the round as you would like to play it. This doesn't mean visualizing shots you can't hit. It means seeing the shots you know you can hit, because you know your game is good enough to win. All you have to do is let yourself play it. You imagine yourself standing on the tee of a hole that doesn't set up well to your eye. Imagine yourself taking a 3-wood or an iron to get the ball into play. Imagine the speed of the greens. See yourself being firm on slow greens, knocking the ball into the back of the cup. See your putts dying in the hole on fast greens.

Good players have always had a knack for visualization, even if they never consulted a sports psychologist. Nicklaus, as I've said, spoke of movies in his head. He would stand over a putt for as long as it took for the movie to show the ball going into the hole. To spectators, it appeared that he could "will" the ball into the hole. In a sense, that's what he was doing.

Sam Snead once told me that when he was in his prime, he used to take a shower and climb into bed at night. Before he fell asleep, he'd replay the day's round in his mind. Except that wherever he'd made a bad shot, he would "erase" it and see himself playing a great shot instead. When he woke up the next morning, he'd head off to the course with a tune on his lips and a spring in his step, as confident as he could be that he was going to have a great round. As often as not, he did.

Visualization can help to make up for a lack of experience. Most of us get nervous when we're thrust into a situation that's new and unknown. You've played your home course many times, but if you've never played it in a tournament, that's a new and unknown situation. On the professional level, you may have played many Sunday rounds, but if you've never played in the final group at a major championship, that's a new and unknown situation.

But this sort of situation is less a step into the darkness if you've successfully visualized it in advance. Visualization can give you a comforting déjà vu feeling about a clutch situation. Tiger Woods sometimes says that on the last day of a major championship, in contention, he feels he has an advantage over a lot of his rivals because he's been through the experience before. Visualization can help players feel as Tiger does, that they've been there, they've come through it, and there's nothing to be worried about.

10.

Perception

Golfers generally don't become my clients because they've just had a series of satisfying experiences in clutch situations. They usually look me up after they've gotten into a clutch situation and, as one of my clients liked to put it, thrown up all over themselves.

That feeling is a normal part of golf. Golf is difficult. No matter how much you practice and how skilled you become, there are going to be moments, sometimes whole days, when you hit the ball sideways. There are going to be days when you fall short of your best. It's a game that seems almost to have been designed to cause angst.

If you play competitive golf, there are certainly going to be days when you find yourself in a clutch situation and lose. There are going to be days when you find yourself in a clutch situation and play badly—or at least feel that you did. So learning to deal with failure is, perhaps paradoxically, one of the challenges of developing and maintaining the confidence that leads to success.

In dealing with these situations, I try to help players see that what's important is not so much what happened to them. It's how they decide to perceive what happened. It's how they interpret or explain it to themselves. It's the meaning they choose to assign to it.

I'm not talking about putting on a pair of rose-colored glasses and deluding yourself here. There's no point in pretending that failure is success. I am talking about seeing your performance realistically. I am talking about learning from mistakes. I'm talking about using a bad experience as a stepping-stone that will lead to a better result in the future.

Let's consider a hypothetical young golfer on the PGA Tour. He's been touted as someone with lots of potential. Maybe he's won a regular tournament or two. But he's never won, or been close to winning, a major. And it's always been his dream to win one or more of them.

Our player goes to a major championship hitting the ball well. His game is clicking. The course is devilishly hard, but for the first three days, he handles it. He's a good putter, and he's got the feel of the greens. He's got a great short game, and he's getting up and down a lot. He's not driving it into every fairway; no one does at a major, where the ground is usually firm and even a well-struck tee shot can hit a dry, hard mound and carom into grass so deep and thick you can't see your shoes when you address your next shot. Our player copes well with all of these things and finds himself, after fifty-four holes, in the lead by a shot. Not only that. He's paired on Sunday with someone he's idolized—with Tiger, perhaps, or with Phil or Ernie.

After he signs his third-round card, nothing that happens is similar to anything he's experienced before. He goes to the pressroom and has to re-create his life history for the foreign journalists who have never heard of him. He hears innumerable questions that all try to get him to say that he feels like a novice skier who's made a wrong turn onto an expert slope and can't turn back. Then he goes back to his hotel room and tries to relax, but he can't sleep. He gets up the next day feeling tired and groggy. He won't be teeing off until 2 P.M., so he passes some time watching the cable broadcast of the players who teed off early. He pulls out a pen and a pad to take some notes on how the ball is breaking around the Sunday hole locations, but all he seems to notice is that all the holes are on knobs or next to bunkers, and the greens all look treacherously fast. It's a relief when he finally goes to the course to warm up, but even that doesn't go as planned, because Roger Maltbie wants to ask how he feels about starting with the lead.

On the first hole, he hits what feels like a good tee shot, but he gets one of those bounces, and the ball finds the rough. He can't reach the green with his second. He ever so slightly mishits his pitch on the third shot and the ball rolls fifteen feet past the hole. He desperately wants to save par, and he gives the putt a little more weight than it needs. On the glassy greens, it goes five feet past. Now our player is facing a nasty putt to save bogey, and he can't seem to see the line the way he did on Thursday, Friday, and Saturday. Uncertain, he leaves the putt an inch short. Walking off the green, he looks at a scoreboard and watches his lead officially disappear. His confidence is going, too.

On the second hole, a treacherous, drivable par four, he decides he'd better go for it rather than take an iron, lay up, and try to make birdie with a wedge and a putt. After all, he reasons, he'd played it conservatively the first three days and had only pars to show for it. His drive is a good, long one, and for a moment it looks like it will not only find the green, but stop close to the hole. Unfortunately, it catches a wicked side slope and trickles into a greenside bunker. Our player has short-sided himself, and he's in trouble even though he's only twenty-five feet from the hole. He tries to land his bunker shot precisely on the edge of the green and let it roll down to the hole, but he catches a trifle too much sand and leaves it in the trap. Then he blasts out and winds up forty feet away. Bogey.

The round gets worse from there. On this merciless course, our player feels like nothing he can do will work. He stops hitting the ball freely and starts trying to steer it. He gets hesitant and tentative with his putter. An ugly skein of bogeys ensues, and when he staggers off the course, he signs for an 80. The winner turns out to be someone who shot a modest, plodding, even-par round, and our player realizes that he could have won with only a 72 or 73. Then, before he can catch his breath, he's summoned to the media center to explain what happened.

Don't feel sorry for our player. I don't. He's a professional golfer by choice, and all of this goes with the territory. There is a long list of players who took the lead into the final round of a major and shot 80. Ken Venturi and Mike Weir come to mind. They, of course, went on to win majors. And that's the objective. Training your perception will help you achieve it.

The first thing a player has to realize after a disaster is that it's up to him how he perceives what happened. He can choose to make something constructive happen. Or he can choose to turn that 80 into a millstone, hang it around his neck, and let it weigh him down for the rest of his career. In order to do that, all he has to do is succumb to the sorts of thoughts that will either come to him naturally or be suggested to him by the media:

"I'm a choker, I'm not cut out for tournament golf. I don't have what it takes."

Those kinds of all-encompassing negative thoughts are lethal. If a player buys into them, he might as well start looking for a nice teaching job at a club somewhere, because anyone with that mentality will not succeed in tournament golf. You have to find other ways to perceive what happened.

I've known players who encountered disaster and faced it by deciding that something was wrong with their mechanics. Tom Kite blocked a shot into the water in the 1988 U.S. Open. He decided that he needed to revamp his swing to use the big muscles of his body to square the clubhead, on the theory that in the clutch, they were more reliable than hand action. This was not an easy decision for a player immersed in competitive golf to make. It was especially risky because Tom was a very successful player, and there was no guarantee that a revamped swing would work for him. But Tom has never been afraid of practice. He worked assiduously on his new mechanics for the better part of two years, and in 1992 he won the Open.

There might be a mechanical flaw behind anyone's poor shot under pressure. Maybe you're a player who tends to flip or scoop his chips and pitches. At the club championship, maybe you bladed one or chunked one at a critical juncture. If you look back on your performance and decide that competition exposed the flaw in your short-game mechanics, then by all means go see your pro, take a lesson or two, and practice until you have sound mechanics.

I've known players who responded to unsuccessful clutch performances by blaming their equipment, their caddies, their swing coaches. I've heard stories about players who broke their putters. A legendary old player named Ky Laffoon reportedly got so mad at his putter that he tied it to the bumper of his car and dragged it to the next tournament. The putter deserved it, he said. Nowadays, since players rarely drive from tournament to tournament, he'd probably have to be content with leaving the offending implement on an airport luggage carousel and switching to a belly putter.

I'll say one thing for players who react to a loss by blaming their equipment or firing their caddies: They're better off than players who castigate themselves. If you blame your caddie, at least you're not filling your mind with thoughts about how *you* can't play clutch golf.

But to be realistic about it, a player in the situation I described earlier needs to begin with the fact that after three rounds, he led the tournament. That doesn't mean he should have won it, necessarily. It does mean that for three rounds, his swing, his equipment, his caddie, and everything else performed at a high level. If you've gone through several rounds of match play to get to the playoffs of your club's member-guest and your chipping was fine until the playoffs, that doesn't suggest you have a mechanical flaw.

This is encouraging. It means you have the tools. Not every player does. So the first thing I'd say to a player who lost the lead in the final round of a major or hit an embarrassing shot in the playoffs at the member-guest, is, "Good work! You didn't finish the job, but you proved you can do it. The next day or two will be critical. It's how you react to what happened today that will determine whether you get into this situation again and how well you'll perform when you do."

People who have won major championships sometimes talk about the importance of experience. And it's true that many players, like Padraig Harrington, seem to follow a pattern of coming close a few times in big events, then finally getting over the hump. You can habituate yourself to clutch pressure. But in my experience, that happens only when a player perceives what happened to him constructively.

The player who reacts constructively will not try to evade his responsibility for the outcome. He will ask himself some tough questions:

Did I have the right attitude before every shot?

Did I give each shot on Sunday the same relatively low level of importance that I was giving each shot on Thursday?

Was I focused on my target, on where I wanted the ball to go? Or did I start looking at the scoreboard, thinking about the tournament standings, about likely outcomes or swing mechanics or any of a thousand other things that are not helpful on the golf course?

Did I stick with my routine?

Was I decisive?

If a player can answer "yes" to these questions, then all he needs to do is shrug and assume that the breaks of the game will someday even out. In a crucible of pressure, he has played like a confident champion. His time will come.

I think back to the way Jim Furyk and Tiger Woods reacted after they lost the 2007 U.S. Open to Angel Cabrera. Both of them made mistakes on the short, par-four 17th hole in the final round. Neither of them castigated himself for it.

Furyk said he'd selected the right club, his driver. He figured that he might not reach the green, but if he missed, he'd leave himself in position to chip it close to the hole and make a birdie or at worst a par. He'd hit the ball well. He just hit it twenty yards farther than he'd done on previous days. He'd found a patch of rough that was one of the longest, thickest, and nastiest at Oakmont, which is analogous to picking a fight with the toughest, meanest guy in a Navy SEALs unit. He had a bad angle to the hole, he wound up making bogey, and his chance of winning the Open effectively ended.

Reporters asked him to second-guess himself. He refused. "The play I made was the play," Furyk said. "Now if I went back, I wouldn't hit left of the green for damn sure. But, no, it was the play. I would stick by that play through and through with the way the wind conditions were and the pin position was. In my mind, I made the right decision. I shouldn't have hit the ball so far left, but I'm surprised it went as far as it did.

"I'm proud of the way I played. But, you know, second is not that much fun, to be honest with you."

This is a good example of the way a confident champion perceives a mistake in the clutch. He asks himself whether he made the right decisions, had the right attitude, and executed well. If he believes he did, he can accept the result with equanimity. That doesn't mean he's happy about losing, as Furyk said. But he's not going to let it disturb his confidence.

Woods played 17 with a 3-wood, which found one of the hole's many bunkers. His bunker shot rolled over the green and into the rough on the other wide. He had to make a six-foot putt to save par, but he'd needed a birdie to catch Cabrera.

When he was asked about it, Woods, like Furyk, declined to blame himself.

"I hit a nice bunker shot but unfortunately when I hit it, I could tell it caught a rock on my wedge. And I heard a 'cling,' you know? And when it came out, I was hoping, 'Please, still have the spin on it,' but it didn't. It released on through. And I had a pretty easy chip. Tried to make it; didn't. But then I had a hard putt again, and I made that one."

I don't know if there really was a rock in that bunker, but I know that Woods's response is typical of a champion's perception of a shot that didn't work in the clutch. It shows the sort of thinking that helps a player walk away from a tough loss and still feel absolutely confident he can win the next big tournament.

In their minds, Woods and Furyk had asked themselves the tough questions. Did they have the right attitudes? Did they play decisively? Did they focus on their targets and did they stick with their routines? When they were able to answer "yes," they were satisfied. Not happy, but satisfied.

However, if a player's answers to some of those tough questions are "no," then there are things to learn. Where and why did his mental focus break down? What can he do to make sure it doesn't happen again?

One thing I often counsel players to do is resist the temptation to look at scoreboards. This is not something an amateur generally needs to worry about, but the amateur has an analogous distraction in his back pocket—the scorecard. It's generally better for a professional to forget about the scoreboard and focus on his targets and his routine. It's generally better for an amateur to forget what he's shooting or where the match stands and to focus on the same things.

Often, the answer for the golfer is simply to rededicate himself to the sound principles and practices that he's already learned. Everyone slips sometimes. Under tournament stress, it's easier to slip than it is during a casual round for a $2 Nassau.

But I don't advocate taking too much time for this review. Learn what there is to learn. Maybe jot down a few things that you want to work on in the future. This process should take half an hour. You don't want to spend a lot of time brooding about what happened.

After your constructive review, the best thing to do about your bad experience is to forget it.

Yes, I know. It's easier to say that than it is to do it.

But great clutch players manage to do this. Ken Bowden, the writer who coauthored Jack Nicklaus's autobiography, has told me that he had an easy time getting Jack to reminisce about the eighteen professional majors that he won. Jack could recall all of the critical shots in great detail. But Jack couldn't remember much about the nineteen times he finished second in majors. Particularly if he finished second because he'd stumbled down the stretch, he had few, if any, memories. It wasn't that Jack didn't want to remember. He was well past his playing prime when he published this autobiography, so he had nothing to lose by being forthright. In Jack's typical, assiduous fashion, he wanted to do a thorough, professional job on the book. He just didn't remember. No sports psychologist had advised Jack to forget his losses. There were no sports psychologists when he was in his prime. Jack just figured out, or instinctively knew, that it would do him no good to harbor bad memories. So he let them go.

I have had players tell me that they can't let go, they can't help but revisit the memories of bad clutch shots. They have nightmares about them. So I realize that not all golfers can let bad memories go as easily and instinctively as Jack did.

The trick lies in two things I've already mentioned.

One is that you must learn not to get overly emotional about bad shots, no matter where or when they occur. Strong emotion associated with an event is like heat: It sears the memory into your brain. So when you get angry or upset about a bad shot, you're making its repercussions worse. One reason you might get overly emotional about a bad shot is that you're investing too much intensity in it. Remember that good clutch players tend to give each shot of their lives the same relatively low level of importance—an intensity you might describe as three to four on a ten-point scale. They're into their targets. They want their shots to go to their targets. But they know that regardless of how the shot comes off, they're going to find the ball and hit it again and keep doing that until the round or the tournament is over. They can accept whatever happens. Even though they've dreamt about winning and trained long and hard to prepare to win, they keep golf in perspective. They know that in the final analysis it's just a game. They know that whether they go around in 70 or 80, their world will keep turning. The important people and relationships in their lives will still be there.

I don't think it's a coincidence that Nicklaus, who won more majors than anyone else, always kept his family as his first priority. Some of his competitors might have thought that Jack was making a sacrifice and diminishing his chance to win when he flew off from a tournament site on Friday afternoon, watched a son play high school football, then returned to the tournament on Saturday morning. I don't think it diminished his chances at all. He might have been marginally more tired in the third round because of his travels. But putting a high priority on his family, I suspect, helped keep his mind and attitude where they needed to be for long-term success.

Similarly, if you want to control your memory, you need to adopt a cool attitude toward what you do on the golf course. Again, think of a meter with a needle that you keep in the medium-cool range, around three or four on a scale of ten, regardless of the situation.

I know it can seem contradictory to want something badly enough to spend hours or even a career chasing it, then to be almost indifferent to what happens. But this dichotomy is something we humans can manage. Actors, for instance, know that no matter how fervently they've dreamed about becoming actors, no matter how hard they've worked to prepare and get an opportunity, they have to be professional when the time comes to step on stage or in front of a camera. They have to practice their craft if they want their characters to emerge as they perform. They have to set aside the intensity of their desire to become successful actors. The good ones manage to do that.

If you can do this, I am not saying you will completely and forever forget all the mistakes you make on the golf course. You won't. But the memories will be less frequent and less intense. This will make it easier for you to counteract them with all of the positive thoughts you're going to be feeding your subconscious mind.

Remember that the subconscious self-image is in effect a register of all the thoughts you have about yourself, with the more recent ones counting more than the older ones. No one's self-image is 100 percent positive. Everyone, even Jack Nicklaus, occasionally remembers a failure. But the subconscious self-image is a little like the grades you got in school. You didn't need to score 100 percent to get an A. Ninety or 95 percent would do. It's the same way with memory and the subconscious. A score of 90–95 percent on strong, positive thoughts and memories will do very nicely.

11.

Talking to Yourself

I magine yourself married, if you're not already. Imagine that
your spouse, every night before you went to bed, started to
criticize you.

"You look sloppy," this person would say. "Your breath stinks.
You bored me at dinner tonight with your inane conversation.
You really don't have a very good mind, you know? But it's still
a lot better than your waistline. One thing you can do at dinner
is shovel that food in. And speaking of weight, you're not carrying yours, financially speaking. It's been way too long since you
got a raise. I need things. My brother just bought a new Mer-
cedes, and I've been stuck with this crummy Lexus for years,
thanks to you. I'm embarrassed to drive to the grocery store.
You're really a total failure, you know. And, by the way, don't
touch me tonight. I'm not in the mood."

How long would you continue to love this sort of spouse?
Not very long, I would imagine. If the marriage survived, it
would be a cold one.

Yet while most people would immediately call a lawyer if
their spouses continued to talk this way, many golfers habitually
inflict the same sort of cruelty on themselves at great cost to
their confidence. They do it with their self-talk.

By self-talk, I do not mean the sort of deluded, out-loud maundering of Carl Spackler in *Caddyshack*. I mean the inner monologue that fills our waking hours. We all, consciously or not, do a kind of radio broadcast of our lives.

Some of us realize it, even embellish it and play with it. On the practice green, we're the ones who are consciously thinking, "He's got this six-footer to win the U.S. Open championship. He takes his last look at the target . . . he hits it . . . lovely, smooth stroke . . . the ball is curling, curling . . . and it's in! We have a new U.S. Open champion! What a pressure putt!"

Some of us aren't aware of our self-talk, at least not consciously. But our subconscious minds are very aware of all the thoughts we have and the judgments we make about ourselves throughout the day. All of this self-talk becomes material that helps form our subconscious self-image.

Whether you fall into the "conscious broadcaster" category or you simply have an unconscious narration running through your mind, you need to understand that what you say to yourself influences your confidence. Self-talk can be a great tool for improving confidence, but it can erode confidence just as easily.

You want to be your own cheerleader. You don't want to be that critical needle that pokes holes in your balloon.

Self-criticism can create a losing syndrome. You think that to be "realistic," you've got to criticize yourself, be tough on yourself, push yourself to work harder to attain that perfect swing or putting stroke. So you work hard, and perhaps your skills improve. But in competition, you don't hit it the way you hit it on the range. A poor self-image is to blame. But you see your poor performance as proof that either your skills are still lacking or that you're just no good. After all, who can argue with the fact that you've just missed the cut by three shots? So you begin the cycle again, criticizing yourself, working harder, and doing nothing to enhance your self-image. The next week you miss the cut by five strokes. And so it goes.

The self-critical golfer, as a beginner, may talk to himself about feeling afraid of embarrassment. He may bemoan his own confusion about how to execute shots. He may complain, internally, about the strange equipment. Or he may think to himself, "The people at this golf course are all looking at me and they don't want me here. They can tell I don't belong. God, I wish I wasn't here." The more advanced player talks to himself more frequently about the quality of his play. He never meets his own expectations. After a mediocre shot, he's likely to think, "You blockhead! How could you miss such an easy shot! You've practiced it a hundred times. But in the clutch, you butcher it!"

At whatever stage, the critical self-talk is almost always one-sided. The novice never congratulates himself for having the foresight to check ahead to make sure he meets the dress standards of the club she's playing at. He never suggests to himself that golf is a tough game, that he's doing fairly well for a newbie, that everyone on the course went through the beginning phase, and that true golfers are happy to see a newcomer take up the game. The advanced player never gives herself credit for the good shots she hits. Her attitude after a successful shot is, "Big deal. It's about time. I ought to be able to play that well whenever I want to."

That little critic inside your head influences performance in two ways. He can affect your self-image and self-confidence in the future. And he can have an immediate and destructive impact on your ability to perform in the present

One mistake common to athletes in all sports, including golf, is telling yourself what not to do. Just before the snap of the ball, a quarterback tells himself, "Don't throw an interception." The likelihood increases that he will either throw an incompletion or an interception. A basketball player on the free-throw line says, "Don't miss this one," and the ball clangs off the rim. Just before he swings, a golfer says to himself, "Don't hit it in the water."

Splash.

Two things happen when a golfer tells himself what not to do. He makes himself more nervous and anxious, because he's thrust the possibility of an error into his mind. His muscles tighten up. He loses his grace and rhythm. And he increases the possibility of hitting exactly the shot he's warned himself not to hit. It sometimes can seem that the brain doesn't understand words like "Don't."

Alternatively, the golfer can respond to this kind of self-talk by making the opposite mistake, in an exaggerated way. The player who tells himself "Don't hook it," hits a block-slice that goes into the woods on the right.

Golfers with sound preshot routines avoid this flaw by focusing consistently and exclusively on what they want to do, rather than what they don't want. They begin by picking out a small target. Suppose you're a 5-iron distance from the green, and the first 100 yards or so are over a pond. As part of your routine, you focus on the flag or on some other target if you're not aiming for the flag—maybe a tree behind the green. Your self-talk, if you say anything to yourself at all, is something like, "Hit it *there.*" You don't let the possibility of going into the water or into a bunker enter your mind.

You may ask, "How can you play smart golf if you ignore the hazards on the course?"

The answer is that you don't ignore them. You account for them in your preround planning. Suppose you're playing a par five with water all down the left side of the hole, curling right up against the green. Well before you start your round, you may tell yourself, "If I put my drive into position where I can reach that green in two, I am going to aim at the tree behind the right half of the green, no matter where the hole is." When you're on the course, you do precisely that. You don't tell yourself, "Don't hit it in the water." You tell yourself, "Aim at the tree."

Particularly on the course, golfers have to become adept at monitoring their self-talk, just as they monitor all their thoughts about the game. If they find themselves thinking, "Don't three-putt," they have to stop themselves. They may even decide to use the word "Stop" in their self-talk, or imagine a stop sign or a police whistle blowing. They can adopt another word as a cue for the right kind of self-talk. Maybe they'll tell themselves, "Easy," or "Let's go." They then remember to say, "Roll it into the hole."

That last bit of self-talk is important. You want it to be focused on the target. If you're about to tee off and you tell yourself, "Take it back slow, make a full turn, keep the wrists firm at the top, start the downswing by bumping the hips a little, then crush it toward that steeple in the distance," you're telling yourself positive things. That's better than saying, "Don't hit it in the bunker." But good golfers don't let their self-talk drift very far into technique and mechanics. They may have a single, consistent swing thought, like "slow tempo." Their self-talk almost always focuses on either that one simple mechanical idea or on their target. The tournament players who win generally are able to eliminate even that single swing thought. They may well think about mechanics while they're preparing for an event. But once competition starts, they strive to talk to themselves only about their targets.

I say "strive" because no one is perfect in his self-talk. Bobby Jones recalled standing over an eighteen-inch putt to win the 1926 U.S. Open and thinking the worst possible thoughts. Jones had rallied on the last eleven holes that day to catch and surpass Joe Turnesa, the third-round leader. He knew exactly where he stood and what the putt meant. At the critical moment, he thought, "What if I stub my putter into the ground and miss the ball entirely and lose the tournament?"

Jones didn't do that, of course. But before he stroked that putt, he did what any good athlete does. He stopped. He backed away from the ball. He got control of his mind, collecting himself until his head was filled with visions of the ball going into the back of the cup. Then he set up and putted the ball into the hole.

I know that there are diligent golfers who will read this and think, "Well, yes. You want to think confidently in competition. But if you're not critical of yourself, how do you improve?"

They have a point. You don't get better unless you identify your weaknesses and practice until they become, if not strengths, at least not liabilities. If you play a round in which you hit just a few fairways, or three-putt several greens, you're not going to score well. An intelligent approach to the game dictates that if you want to improve, you realize that you need to work on being more accurate off the tee or putting better. A competitive player will do that. But the time to evaluate and criticize your performance is not during the round. During the round, if you're talking to yourself, you want to be applauding yourself for your good shots and thinking about executing your game plan, thinking about targets and where you want the ball to go. Afterward, you'll have time to figure out what you need to work on. And, as you think about it, talk to yourself in positive terms. "I am going to get better with my driver," or "I am going to free myself up and putt to make every putt," are better thoughts than "I'm lousy off the tee." Concentrate on what needs to be corrected rather than thinking of yourself as the one who needs correction.

You must be careful about the self-talk habits you develop. As a coach and an adviser to coaches, I've worked with players who are in the habit of being self-critical. This kind of athlete often seems to be the sort that every coach wants on his team. Harsh self-critics take practice very seriously. They're often great practice players.

But in competition, this habit of critical self-talk serves them poorly. They find it hard to trust themselves and their skills. If they get a lead, they start to think about blowing it. They worry and envision catastrophe. If they make an error, they find it hard to shrug it off and keep playing. They brood about it. They forget that all athletes make mistakes and perfection is not a prerequisite for success. In the clutch, they're tight. They find it difficult to relax, play confidently, and let their skills manifest themselves.

Your self-talk also influences your golfing comfort zone. You now know that the subconscious can regulate your golf the way a thermostat regulates the temperature in your home, kicking the furnace or the air-conditioning to life when the temperature goes above or below certain limits. If your self-talk is consistently critical, your subconscious will make it hard to keep cruising along at three under par. It will think that you instead want to be the bumbler that you're always accusing yourself of being. It will try to help you make enough bad shots to get there. If you're the sort of player who periodically gets off to a great start but can't sustain it, who winds up shooting 85 whether your front nine is 37 or 47, you might want to think carefully and candidly about your self-talk.

Conversely, if your self-talk is consistently encouraging, it can help you through a bad patch during a round of golf. You might make a few bogeys, get some bad breaks, and find yourself in difficulty. If your subconscious mind believes "I'm better than this," it will help you get back on track.

Athletes in team sports have an advantage over golfers when it comes to self-talk. For one, they practice and play under the close supervision of a coach or manager. Good coaches and managers are experts at telling players what their psyches need to hear. Successful coaches know how and when to criticize a player. They may do it harshly. But good coaches tend to do it well before it's time for their teams to perform. In the final stages of preparation, they're about building up their players' confidence. In the face of the inevitable setbacks during the course of a season, the coach can become a kind of lightning rod, absorbing the worst of his players' frustration. Instead of thinking critically about themselves, they think critically of the coach. That's why you'll usually see the best coaches taking the blame for a loss on themselves and absolving their players. Finally, at least in some sports and in some positions, a coach can motivate his players by giving them a pep talk, by exhorting them to try harder. If you're a defensive lineman, trying harder may well work.

But it probably won't if you're a golfer. Golfers may have swing teachers (and psychologists) to advise them from time to time. But for the most part, they're alone. They can't receive coaching during a round except from their caddies. (This is why a good caddie is worth the share of his player's earnings that he receives. The good caddies that I've observed all have a knack for telling their players what they need to hear at a critical juncture.) Though they can replace their caddies, golfers have a harder time getting angry at someone else when they play badly. The likelihood, after all, is that neither the caddie, nor the psychologist, nor the swing teacher instructed them to drive a ball into the woods on the 72nd hole. And golfers can't fall back on the strategy of simply exhorting themselves to try harder. If you try harder during a round of golf, try to *force* yourself to hit good shots, you're likely to play worse instead of better. So if you're a golfer, developing the ability to talk to yourself in the right away is doubly important. Your self-talk has to replace what athletes in other sports hear from coaches. It has to remind you quietly and coolly of where you want to hit the ball and to remind you that, yes, you can indeed hit it there.

Off the course, it's another matter. What you hear from others has an effect on your subconscious. It's your job to make sure you surround yourself with people who tell you the right things.

If you're a professional golfer or a competitive amateur, you'll want to surround yourself with cheerleaders. I'm not talking about people who are unfailingly Pollyannaish. But you don't need someone to tell you that you played badly, or you have a tough opponent coming up, or that you probably don't have the genes to be a good putter. You need people in your life who will be supportive in all cases and constructive when they offer advice.

You don't need companions who are constantly whining and groaning about their games, the golf course, or anything else. There's a reason that Harvey Penick advised young Tom Kite to always seek out good putters for his dinner companions. He didn't want Tom listening to people griping about the speed of the greens or the quality of the turf or anything else.

I know that among friends who play together regularly, there's a lot of needling. But there's a difference between some friendly teasing over a $2 bet and a constant barrage of negative remarks about anyone's golf game. The best golf companions, in my experience, are the ones who choose to say nothing or to say things that are encouraging and complimentary. If you're not playing with people like that, maybe you ought to consider reconfiguring your regular Saturday foursome.

12.

The Cradle
of Your Confidence

When I work with players who tell me that their scores do not reflect their talents, I often take out a piece of paper and ask them to go through a recent unsatisfactory competitive round, shot by shot. I make a chart that indicates the club the player used for each stroke in the round and the distance the player had to the hole. When it's done, the chart usually points to something that's vitally important to both scoring and confidence. If you're a good player, you probably already know what I'm talking about.

The short-game shots, the ones you hit with anything from an 8-iron to a putter, are the ones that most often determine how well you'll score. It's great to be able to drive the ball 300 yards and still better to be able to drive it 300 yards straight. I certainly advocate being able to do it. I advocate devoting a reasonable amount of your practice and preparation to it. But unless you play well with the short-game clubs, your long drives won't do you much good on the scorecard.

Not long ago, I spent some time with a college golfer, a kid with tremendous potential. We went over a round in which he'd shot 75. We established that fourteen of those seventy-five shots were tee shots on par fours and fives. Not all of his tee shots hit the fairway, but none of them got him into trouble, by which I mean that none left him in such a bad spot that he had to waste a shot to put the ball back into play. Another eight of his shots were long irons or fairway woods. No fewer than fifty-three of the seventy-five were hit with the 8-iron, 9-iron, wedge, and the putter. Thirty-four were putts.

We analyzed his score further. He had missed six greens. Of those six chances he had to get the ball up and down, he converted one. He had thirteen occasions when he played his shot into a green with a short iron or a wedge. Out of those thirteen opportunities, he made no birdies.

"Suppose," I said, "that you'd converted half of your up-and-down chances. Suppose you'd made birdie five of the thirteen times you had a short-iron approach shot. What would your score have been?"

It didn't take long for him to do the math. "Sixty-eight," he said.

In a college golf tournament, the difference between 75 and 68 is enormous. Seventy-five means you're dragging your team down. Sixty-eight means you're helping your team and in contention for individual honors.

"So how much time do you spend practicing your tee shots and how much time do you spend on your short game?" I asked the kid.

He blushed.

I conduct the same kind of scorecard review with professional players in a slump. In their cases, the numbers may be a little lower. But the principle remains the same. If you're not scoring well, the reason very likely is your play with the short irons or the putter.

A lot of players are quick to believe that their putters are the problem. "I'm just not making anything," they'll say.

It could be. But in my observation, the problem lies as frequently with the short irons and wedges as it does with the putter. I had a session recently with a client who's always been a fine putter. He didn't think he was putting well. But when we looked more closely at his recent play, we found that his birdie putts, when he had them, were coming from an average of thirty feet or more. No one makes a lot of putts from that range.

In fact, I'd be happy to make a wager for a substantial sum on a ten-putt contest. I'll let you pick any putter in the world you want for your side. You can have Tiger, Brad Faxon, Aaron Baddeley—anyone you like. I'll take a guy at random off the practice green at your local golf course. But my guy will putt from four feet and your guy will putt from ten. I guarantee you that the average golfer is going to hole more putts from four feet than the best putter in the world will hole from ten.

So when I go over a disappointing scorecard with a player, I zero in on the data that show how close to the hole he was hitting his wedges and short irons. If he wasn't knocking them close—inside ten feet from 100 yards out in the fairway, inside three feet from around the green—then the problem isn't his putting. It's his wedge play.

I don't care if we're talking about a club player whose goal is to break 90 or a Tour player who wants to win major championships. The first priority has to be getting good with those clubs. It stands to reason. My dad is well into his eighties and still plays as much golf as he can. He's had some shoulder problems, though, and he can't hit the ball far enough to reach most par-four greens in two shots. A younger player in my dad's handicap range might be long enough to reach any par four in two, but not straight enough. The outcome is the same. They are both going to be hitting wedges into most greens for their third shots. Can they get it on the green, somewhere within two-putt range? If so, they'll probably shoot in the low 90s or high 80s. Can they wedge it close enough to make a putt one-third of the time? Now we're talking about scores in the mid to low 80s. Can they get it close enough to get up and down half the time? Now we're talking about the Promised Land for most amateurs—a single-digit handicap and scores in the 70s.

When I started working with golfers, my experience in sports psychology came primarily from a couple of team sports, basketball and lacrosse. I had learned an essential truth from them. In basketball, the teams that win consistently are not the teams with brilliant shooters, because all shooters are going to have off nights. The consistent winners are the teams that understand the importance of defense, making free throws, and rebounding. You don't have off nights on defense or under the boards. If you dedicate yourself to learning them and practicing them, those skills are always there for you if you're willing to hustle. It's the same way in lacrosse. The best teams are not always the ones with flashy midfielders who have blinding speed and a dozen juke moves. They're the teams that consistently excel at playing defense, at face-offs, at getting to loose balls. Every sport has some skills that don't make highlight reels but pay off big. They're skills that show up consistently, game after game. I looked for the equivalent skills in golf.

They are, without doubt, the shots with the short irons and the wedges. You may not always have your swing in order. The driver will not always behave. You may not always have a good feel for the greens and your putts may not always drop. But you can always score if you can chip, lob, pitch, and hit bunker shots. And though you may have an occasional off day with your wedge game, it will be there for you much more consistently than the perfect full swing.

Of the four basic short-game shots, the pitch is by far the most important. Chipping is helpful and used to be more so. But the truth is that most golf courses, especially tournament courses, are so well kept these days that it's possible to putt from within a few paces of the green, provided you're not in the rough. The number of times you have to play the classic chip shot is diminishing. A great lob shot is the equivalent of the whipped cream on your banana split. It's a nice touch, but it's not always necessary. I see fewer lobs on Tour than I used to. Most players have decided that the percentages, especially from a tight lie, favor a more conventional pitch shot. A good bunker game, obviously, is essential to scoring. On any tough course, you're likely to be in a few greenside bunkers during the course of a round, and your score will be directly affected by how often you manage to get up and down. But, as with chipping, advances in golf course maintenance have diminished the priority I would give to perfecting bunker shots. It used to be that a tournament golfer might need to hit five or six variations of the standard bunker shot in the course of a single round. That was because the condition of the sand varied from hole to hole and bunker to bunker. Nowadays, on the PGA Tour, the sand is virtually the same, not only from hole to hole, but from course to course. Players need just one basic greenside shot. (It's played, of course, from different lies—uphill, downhill, and so on.) Your course's bunkers might not be maintained as well as those on a course hosting a Tour event, but they're still probably a lot better to play from than they were ten or twenty years ago.

At the same time, today's courses place a growing premium on being able to pitch the ball well. By pitch, I mean a shot struck with a wedge or short iron, hit with a downward blow and usually hit with backspin. It flies longer than it rolls. More and more these days, architects are trying to defend par against the onslaught of new equipment by toughening up the greens and the areas that surround them. You see more elevated greens than you used to. You see more front bunkers. You see more greens with tiers or other features that demand a shot that hits a specific target area and stops. All of these shots require pitches.

If your pitching, bunker play, and chipping are not what they ought to be, you need to improve them. The shot diary I've referred to will help you figure out precisely which shots you need to emphasize in your practice. And maybe it's simply a question of devoting some practice time to them. Every good tournament player I know devotes a significant amount of his practice time to wedge play. At the Tour level, players want to have a variety of pitches for different situations, with different trajectories and differing degrees of backspin. They work on them constantly. I advise professional clients to seek out different, vexing lies when they practice, rather than simply clip balls off the uniform turf of the range. I like to see them practice from dirt, from grass so thick and long that they can barely see the ball, and from everything in between. They should work from uphill lies, downhill lies, and sidehill lies—anything a golf course architect can dream up to defend a green. Practicing that way does all the good things we've talked about for a player's confidence. It gives him positive impressions and memories. It feeds his subconscious self-image the notion that he's got a short game that can get the ball up and down from anywhere. In competition, when he encounters a quirky lie on a shot to a tight pin, this confidence serves him well.

I should mention that I have one client who doesn't spend a lot of time around the practice green working on his short game yet is still successful. He's Dana Quigley, who's taken advantage of the second chance he got when he turned fifty to make more than $13 million on the Champions Tour. Dana's approach to the short game is simply to play thirty-six or even fifty-four holes of golf a day. He tells me this gives him the chance to practice the full gamut of wedge shots, from full swings to three-quarters to delicate greenside pitches. And, he gets to do it under conditions that more closely approximate tournament conditions. I can't argue with Dana's results. So if you're reading this and you have the time and stamina to play thirty-six to fifty-four holes of golf a day, you have my blessing if you want to cut back on your short-game practice.

If you don't have that kind of time and stamina, you might want to learn from one of my first mentors in the game of golf, the late, great Paul Runyan. Paul was a wisp of a man, maybe

5'6" and 130 pounds in his prime, who nevertheless managed to win two PGA championships and a money title back in the 1930s. He did it largely with a great short game. One of my favorite shots in golf history was a chip Paul made in the PGA championship finals against Sam Snead. Snead putted so that his ball was between Paul's ball and the hole. In those days, that was called a "stymie," and it might have meant that Paul would have to take two putts to get around Sam's ball and into the hole. Instead, Paul took a niblick and chipped his ball over Sam's ball and into the hole. That's how good he was. In practice, Paul used to take ten balls and drop them in various locations around the practice green, so that he'd have to play every shot in his repertoire. His goal was to get them all holed in fewer than twenty strokes. Most of the time, he did it easily. I love this drill. It simulates real, competitive conditions. It builds confidence. If you can manage to do it in twenty strokes or better, you'll know you have a good short game.

If you practice and don't seem to get better, it's possible that your short game deficiencies are a matter of technique rather than effort. If so, you'll have to find a teacher who can work with you on your short-game mechanics. It's important that this teacher be skilled in short-game instruction. It's important that you meet him around a practice green (not on a driving range) and devote your lesson or lessons to short-game shots.

Keep in mind that it's not uncommon for a player to get a little lost during this process. Each of us has a different learning style. Each of us has a different body. There is no single way to play short-game shots (though good short-game players have a lot in common) and no single way to teach them. It may take a while for you to find a teacher and a method that suit you. You must simply be patient. Once you've selected a teacher you believe in, commit yourself to the method he or she gives you. Stick with it. Practice it. Sooner or later, you will see the results in your scores.

Review your routine with wedges in your hand. You might be the sort of player who has a solid putting routine. You see the target and you let the stroke go. But with wedges, you worry about making solid contact. You don't think about the target. You have to make your wedge-game routine more like your putting routine. See it and hit it.

If you're already sticking your wedges close but you're not scoring, then the problem could lie with your putting. Putting is to golfing confidence what corporate profits are to the stock market. When you're putting well, it's easy to be confident about your whole game. When you're not putting well, it's hard to believe you can score.

Of all the golf shots, putting is probably the one where the mind plays the greatest role. Of course, you read about the ideal putting stroke. There are people writing long books about the mechanics of putting. Scotty Cameron, who makes putters for Titleist, has a testing lab that would do credit to the National Aeronautics and Space Administration. I respect their work, and I understand that it's probably better to have a smooth, optimal stroke than a motion that weaves the putter face around the intended line like an inebriated driver at a sobriety checkpoint.

But I have also seen a client, Billy Mayfair, beat Tiger Woods in a playoff to win the Nissan Open, using a putting stroke that made TV commentators and putting gurus cringe. He took the blade back outside the line of the putt, brought it back from the outside, and looked like he was going to pull everything to the left. But at the last instant, Billy would use his hands to square the blade so it was perpendicular to his intended line. It was the way he'd learned to putt as a kid, on a public course in Phoenix called Papago Park. And it worked for him as long as he believed in it. So I know you don't need perfect putting mechanics to putt well.

You need, first, to decide that you like putting. If you're the sort of player who thinks that golf ought to reward the full-swing shots more and putts less, then you're not likely to be a good putter. As great as he was, when Ben Hogan started grumbling that putts ought to count as only half strokes, he was pretty much done as a competitive golfer. Good putters take pleasure in the fact that so much of golf depends on putting. They love the way it tests their nerves and their imagination. They look at the putting green as a chance to shine, not as an unfair test that for some arbitrary reason they have to pass.

You must also realize that putting is a simple, manageable movement, at least in comparison to the mechanics of hitting a 320-yard power fade with a 7-degree driver. You may not have the clubhead speed for hitting 320-yard power fades. But there's no question that you've got the strength and coordination to roll the ball across a putting green. This means that virtually anyone can learn to putt. Some people may start out with certain advantages, such as keen vision or an instinctive ability to aim. But anyone can learn to putt. If you believe that good putters are born, not made, you have to change your attitude.

Whatever your putting style, you need to practice seeing the ball go into the hole. I find that good putters don't spend a lot of their practice time trying long putts they're not likely to make. They may work on their touch with long putts, but they do it by putting at the fringe of the green or at a tee stuck in the ground. When they putt at a hole, they putt from a range that allows them to make lots of putts, to see the ball go into the hole.

One way to do this is to put a chalk line down on a flat segment of the green, extending outward from a hole. Putt along the chalk line. Watch the ball go in. Dottie Pepper showed me a simple drill that's quite similar. It also requires finding a hole at a place on the putting green where there's no break. Stick a tee in the ground three feet away, another five feet away and a third seven feet away. Putt three straight into the hole from three feet. Move back to five feet and make three in a row. Then move back to seven feet and make three in a row. If you miss a putt, start over from three feet. Don't stop until you have made the nine consecutive putts.

Not only will these drills help groove your stroke. They will cause you to see many, many balls fall into the hole. Every ball that goes in feeds that subconscious self-image. You'll find that the next time you play, you'll look at a five-foot putt and think, "Piece of cake. I know I can hit it where I aim it."

You'll need to check your putting routine to be sure it's helping you. There are an infinite variety of putting routines. Some players squat behind the ball. Some like to look from behind the hole. Some take practice strokes, some don't. Some take their practice strokes looking at the hole, trying to feel the distance. Some take their practice strokes looking at an imaginary ball. Some plumb-bob. Most don't. Jim Furyk reads the putt, gets over the ball, then steps away and reads it again. Phil Mickelson takes practice strokes from different angles. Your physical putting routine can be equally idiosyncratic. It doesn't matter.

But any good routine incorporates a few key mental elements. First, you must make a decisive read. Some players tell me that when they read a putt they can "see" a line between the ball and the hole, almost as bright as a freshly painted line separating the sides of a highway. Others don't see anything. They just decide which way the ball is going to break and how much. That's fine. People have different styles in sight and perception. The important thing is that you are decisive about your read. You believe in it. You're committed to it.

Remember that you don't have to be as precise in reading a putt as NASA has to be in plotting a space shuttle's trajectory. You don't have to find the single, correct line. On most putts, there are a number of lines that will work, depending on the speed with which you hit the ball. Hit the ball firmly, and it will break less. Hit it softly, and it will break more. Some of the players I counsel like a drill that demonstrates this. They make putts of four or five feet in three different ways from the same spot. One bangs straight into the back of the cup. Another, at medium speed, breaks in slightly. And a third, at slow speed, starts well outside the hole, curls, and plops in as it dies. I recommend trying this practice drill. It will help you understand the way putts break. It will help your imagination and feel. It will help you bring those into play when you putt. Putting is an art, not a science.

Your routine must make you decisive. You can't putt well if you find yourself standing over the ball, about to make your stroke, thinking, "I wonder if I shouldn't play it two balls out to the right instead of one." If you have such thoughts, you simply must step away, take another look at the terrain between your ball and the hole, and keep looking until you've firmly decided on the line you're going to choose.

I find that players can avoid the problem of indecision by learning to rely on their first read. If you've played much golf, your brain has already absorbed a lot of information about putts and how they break. As you walk toward a green, see your ball, and see the hole, your eyes begin to feed your brain data. Without conscious thought, you begin to understand how the putt will behave. By the time you squat down behind the ball, you're fine-tuning this process. It's a bit like the way a photographer fiddles with his lens (or did, back in the days before auto-focus) to make an image sharp in his viewfinder. It's not a long process. The image becomes sharp very quickly. So it is with reading putts. This is your first read.

You rarely do yourself any good if you continue to try to analyze the putt after the instant when the image is clarified, just as the photographer can spoil his shot by continuing to turn the focusing ring in search of a 110 percent clarity that doesn't exist. Yes, once in a while you may see something on the your second or third inspection that proves to be a better read than your first one. You may even be able, once in a while, to set aside your confusion, commit to the second line, and sink the putt. But over the long run, continuing to read after you've made your initial judgment can only lead to more indecision. Indecision ruins putting. You will make more putts, overall, if you develop the habit of making one read, committing to it, and stroking the putt. You may not always have the correct read. But you'll generally be close enough. And a decisive stroke will more often send the ball into the hole.

Your goal as you read the putt is to come up with a small, precise target. If it's a straight putt, that target will be inside the hole—maybe a mark on the back of the cup. If it's a breaking putt, most good putters will pick out a target that's about hole high on the initial line of the putt. In other words, if you think the putt will break a foot to the left, your target will be a spot a foot to the right of the hole. In your mind, every putt you hit should be a straight putt. Some will be affected by slope and gravity more than others.

I don't advocate concerning yourself much about speed as you read the putt. Yes, some putts are uphill. Some putts are downhill. Some putts are both. Your eyes and your brain will account for this without you having to think much about it if you simply focus on getting the ball into the hole. They'll register the slopes and the grain and any other factors. Your mind is more effective than any computer. Let it do its work.

It will be most effective if your routine gives you what I call a clear mind. As you prepare to putt, your mind should be focused only on the target—not the stroke or the putting mechanics or the speed. But you don't want to focus on your target with teeth-grinding intensity. Good putters are a touch nonchalant about it. They focus on the target. They want the ball to go to the target. But they don't let themselves care so much about the outcome of the stroke that they get tight. When they do that, they often find themselves trying to steer the ball rather than letting the stroke go. Good putters realize that only two things can happen when a ball is putted. Either it goes in the hole or it doesn't. In either case, they'll still be there, getting ready to play the next shot in a game they love. The world will continue to turn.

This is in keeping with the generally cool disposition that I've already discussed. Coolness is helpful in a number of ways. It keeps the muscles loose. It keeps the mind calm and focused. It helps prevent searing memories if a shot misses.

I find that good putters' routines are generally deliberate and rhythmic once they stand over the ball. Their tempo is:

Look at the target . . . look at the ball . . . let it go.

If you pause for a long time between the phases of this part of your putting routine, bad things can happen. Doubts can creep into your mind. Tightness can creep into your muscles and nerves.

I often find that clients aren't initially good judges of this part of their putting routines. A lot of them tell me that they already do as I suggest. They look at the target . . . look at the ball . . . let it go. But that's not what I see when I watch them putt.

To help them learn to correct themselves, I ask them to narrate their routines out loud. This is what I often hear:

"Look at the target . . . look at the ball . . . . letitgo."

There's no rhythm to that. Once they're asked to narrate their routines out loud, players realize it. It's a good practice tool to use in improving your routine. You have my permission to murmur so that only you can hear it. You wouldn't want people to think you were talking to yourself on the putting green.

Always putt to make it. There's an old shibboleth in golf that says that on longer putts, you should try merely to "lag" the ball somewhere near the hole or to leave it within a three-foot radius of the hole. Another misleading maxim says there are putts you try to make and . . . well, the purveyors of this maxim never say you try to miss the others, but that's the implication, isn't it? I don't see the logic in either of these ideas. If you're aiming at the smallest target you can see—a spot inside the cup or a blade of grass—you're naturally going to be more accurate than if you're aiming at a three-foot circle. Suppose you aim for the cup and miss by three feet. Won't you be better off than if you aim for a circle around the cup and miss by three feet? And if you're not trying to make a putt, what are you trying to do? Why try to miss?

Of course, you won't try to make every putt roll into the hole in the same way. On an uphill putt, you may be trying to hit the ball firmly, to take any minor break out of the putt, to bang it into the back of the cup. You have the luxury of knowing that the slope behind the hole will stop your ball if you miss and leave you with a tap-in. On a sloping, downhill putt on a fast green, your idea will be different. You don't want to hit the ball firmly enough to make it bang into the cup. You want it to drip in just as it dies. So you hit it softly, playing extra break, because you know that slopes affect a soft putt more than a firm one.

But in either case, you're trying to make it

The final part of a good putting routine is acceptance. Good putters have the ability to think in several seemingly contradictory ways about putting. They have the ability to believe they're going to make every putt they attempt. But if they miss, they have the ability to accept the result and shrug it off. Then they have the ability to believe they're going to make the next one.

You're going to miss some putts. If it were otherwise, the Tour's putting leaders would be taking one putt per green in regulation instead of 1.7 putts. Par would be 54. The best thing to do if you miss a putt, whether it's from one foot or a hundred feet, is to forget about it. Maybe you misread it. Maybe you mishit it. Maybe the green surface was flawed. It doesn't matter. Golf is a game played by human beings, on ground prepared by human beings, so not every putt is going to drop.

If you'd like to aim for a grade of 100 percent in putting, grade yourself this way: Did you follow your mental and physical routine on your putts? Did you believe every putt was going in? Did you roll them with a consistent, low intensity? Were you decisive? If you can answer each of these questions affirmatively about every putt in your round, give yourself 100 percent. It doesn't matter how many actually went in. You've done everything you had the power to control.

If you can do that, it's inevitable that your putting will be one of the strongest parts of your game.

Golfers with good wedge games and good putting games tend to be confident golfers. That's because they know that come what may, they can score. When they step onto the tee, they're not overly concerned with hitting their drives just right. In the fairway, they're not putting excessive pressure on themselves to hit the green and get it close. They certainly aim for a particular spot in the fairway or a particular spot on the green. Quite often, they hit it there. But they remain nonchalant.

Take a cue from Tiger Woods. Based on statistics and past experience, Tiger knows that in any given round, he may not hit a lot of fairways. But he steps on the tee knowing that wherever he hits it, he can still make pars and birdies, because he can get the ball close with his wedges. He can sink putts. He can win. That's a major source of his implacable confidence.

Let it be a source of yours, too.

13.

Nip the Yips

I know of nothing that destroys confidence like a case of the
yips. And, like the flu, here's a lot of it going around these
days.

The yips are nothing new. Ben Hogan, in his forties, used to
stand over the ball so long that he could scarcely draw the putter back. Sam Snead battled the yips for decades, resorting to
"sidesaddle" and "croquet" styles in an effort to stop them
More recently, Bernhard Langer has worked through several
well-publicized bouts with putting yips by going to the belly
putter and then the long putter. As far back as a century ago, the
great Englishman, Harry Vardon, bemoaned his own case: "I
know what it is to feel that I cannot putt . . . to miss the most
absurdly little ones," Vardon wrote. The yips were an affliction
that beset him late in his career, after he'd won his six British
Opens. Had he developed them earlier, he most certainly would
not have compiled the record he did, for he never cured them.
When Vardon became convinced he had the yips, his competitive career was over.

Nowadays, I hear not only about putting yips. Chipping
yips seem to be epidemic. I have clients who tell me that they
quake when they leave themselves a short pitch or a chip from

a tight lie. They're afraid they're either going to skull the ball or chunk it. The former produces a shot that scurries way past the hole, and the latter produces a shot that may move the sod farther than the ball.

People love to talk to me about their yips. The notion that their problems stem from some sort of disease—maybe a virus they picked up when another player sneezed—comforts them. It relieves them of responsibility.

Whether I'm hearing about putting yips or chipping yips, there are some common complaints. The player feels he loses control of his hands as he moves the clubhead toward the ball. If we're talking about the putting yips, he feels like an involuntary spasm of his nervous system causes him to turn the putter blade to the right or left, and the ball never gets on the proper line. With the chipping yips, the golfer perceives that same involuntary spasm, but most often it leads to breaking the wrists and trying to flip the ball into the air instead of hitting down on it. This causes the skulled shot. Once he's worried about that, the player may start trying to compensate and hit the ground before he hits the ball.

Contrary to what I hear so often and you may have heard as well, the yips are not a disease. There is no such neurological condition as the yips. (There are diseases, like Parkinson's, which can cause involuntary tremors. If you have one of them and you're playing golf, you have my admiration. Keep it up and good luck.)

When a player tells me he has the putting yips, for instance, I always ask him which putts they affect. Is it the same for thirty-foot putts as it is for three-foot putts? Usually, the response is, "No, Doc. They only bother me on short putts."

I reply, "Good. Then there's nothing wrong with your body. If there was, it would affect all your putts, not just the short ones. Your problem is you're scared out of your mind."

There is a possibility that golfers have developed the yips, whether on the green or around it, in part because of physical flaws.

For instance, I've seen players who have developed a habit of setting up poorly when they putt. Their putter blades aren't perpendicular to the proper, intended line of the putt. Somewhere in their subconscious brains, they recognize this. They begin compensating with a little twitch of the hands as they bring the blade through and they contact the ball. If they start missing putts, and they get overwrought about it, this twitch can becomes the yips.

But setting up poorly and aiming the blade in the wrong direction are not the yips. Nor do they invariably lead to the yips.

If you think you have a mechanical problem that's causing the putting yips, there's a solution. Find a pro who has one of the devices that clip on your putter and aim a laser at a spot on the wall. This device will tell you if you're really aimed where you think you're aimed. It will help you correct any setup problems you may have. I recommend it. Once you've worked your aiming problem out, your yips should get better—if they're rooted in this mechanical problem.

Physical issues can also contribute to yips in the wedge game. A player might set up poorly, with too much weight on his back foot. Or she doesn't shift her weight during the swing, hanging back on her right side (if she's right-handed). These flaws promote using the hands to flip the ball into the air, rather than hitting down on it and letting the clubface do the work. This can lead to skulled shots and fat shots. After a while, a player can sense that his swing path is flawed and start trying to compensate with his hands just before contact. This usually just exacerbates the problem, and it can be perceived as a case of the yips.

But it's not the yips. The yips are a mental condition, not a mechanical flaw.

If you think you have the yips in your wedge game, it makes sense to see a pro and ask him or her to examine your technique to see if there are mechanical flaws that could be causing inconsistent contact. If so, work with the pro to fix them. Once you've done that, see if the yips go away.

If mechanical improvements to your putting and wedge game don't make the yips go away, it's likely that for you, as with most people afflicted with the yips, the problem and its roots are in your mind. I've mentioned Sam Snead. He never had the yips until he made a winter tour to South Africa in 1946–47, playing a series of exhibitions against Bobby Locke. Nowadays, Locke is recognized as one of the game's all-time greats. But in 1946, he wasn't nearly as well known. Snead was one of the best players in the world, if not the best. In South Africa, though, he suffered a humiliating series of losses; Locke took fourteen of sixteen matches. Worse, Locke beat Snead largely on the greens; Locke was a great putter and Snead didn't have the feel for the varieties of grass grown in South Africa. Under pressure, Snead missed a few critical short putts. He soon began to complain that he had the yips.

Over the next few decades, Snead tried to cope with the

problem by changing putters and changing putting styles. He liked to talk about his yips. He took some comfort from the false notion that aging nerves caused the yips, just as aging eyes begin to have trouble reading a phone book. Maybe that's why Snead never addressed the psychological roots of his yips and thus always had them. Only his brilliant ball striking kept him competing in the top echelons of the game.

We can only guess how good Snead might have been if he had known that the yips are curable. Like ants in an old house, they're not easy to get rid of. But it can be done.

The real source of the yips is pressure, internal pressure that golfers place on themselves. Snead succumbed to this when he found himself losing, unexpectedly, to Bobby Locke. People with the yips fill their minds with thoughts like: "I've got to get this up and down. I absolutely have to sink this. If I don't, it will ruin my score. What will the guys in my group/the people in the gallery/the television audience think of me if I mess up this shot? What will I think of myself? I'll feel terrible!"

Or, if you've been working on the shot that bothers you, it's, "Darn it, I have to make this one, because otherwise I've wasted all that practice time."

Perfectionists tend to be more susceptible to the yips. They not only want to make all their short putts. They want the ball to roll into the middle of the cup and bang against the back at a precise speed. They want their strokes to look perfect, not just get the job done. They're constantly telling themselves that they're not good enough, that they have to get better. When they fail to meet their own expectations, they berate themselves.

Physically, people who think in these ways begin to flinch at the moment of truth. That physical flinching is an expression of their psyche. They flinch at the prospect of investing so much of their egos in the success of a golf shot. They flinch at the prospect of the self-flagellation a miss will cause. That's why players who have the yips on two-foot putts don't have them on thirty-foot putts. They don't expect to make them. They don't fear the emotional consequences of a miss.

This underscores the importance of learning to play golf all the time with the tachometer well below the red line. People who can do that generally don't get the yips. If you haven't experienced the yips and don't want to, this is the way to inoculate yourself against them.

If you've already got the yips, you've got some work to do to get rid of them.

You've taken the first step by reading this far. You understand that the yips reside in your brain, not the neurons around your wrists.

Your next step is to recognize that as you've gotten yourself mired in the yips, you've developed a subconscious self-image that reflects them. You see yourself as a yippy putter or a yippy pitcher of the ball. Your subconscious thinks that's what you want to be.

So one of the first steps in rehabilitating yourself is going to be to work on that subconscious self-image. When you practice or play, make a special effort to remember chips, pitches, and putts that go where you want them to go. Do this for shots both in practice and competition.

Reinforce those memories. Remind yourself to take pleasure in these shots and putts when you pull them off. Get rid of the attitude that "Hmmph. It's about time." When you leave the course, envision the way those shots looked and felt. Relive seeing the ball go in the hole. When you write in your golfing journal, jot down the details. It may seem excessive to you to write down, "Made three-foot curling putt on practice green." It won't seem excessive to your subconscious. It doesn't have that harsh, rigid tendency to judge yourself that you've somehow developed. You need to re-create your self-image so that your subconscious sees you as a great pitcher of the golf ball or a great putter.

Stop telling people you've got the yips. They'd probably rather not hear about it. There's an old saying that half the people in the locker room don't care how you made eight on the first hole and the other half wish you'd made nine. I'm not sure people are that callous, but no good player I know of wants to be around someone who's always moaning about his game. That kind of thinking might be contagious. So if you like talking about your yips, you'll soon very likely be down to an audience of one or two. One will be a player you know who's glad to join the pity party because it gives him a chance to air his own complaints. The other will be your subconscious.

What you need to start saying when you're asked about your game is, "Great."

If someone asks how your putting and chipping are, you can say, "Getting better. I feel good about them."

You're going to have to revamp the mental side of your routine so that, at its core, you simply see where you want the ball to go and hit it there. How do you do this? First, you have to resolve to change. You can also practice the sort of mentality that you're looking for by inventing practice games that push you to focus narrowly on your target.

Tom Kite used to play such a game with his longtime caddie, Mike Carrick. Tom would station Mike a short distance away on the practice range. Mike would pace off various distances, marking them with towels. Then Tom would hit wedges, aiming them directly at Mike. As he did, he'd call out the yardage he thought the ball would travel. Mike would sidestep, catch the ball, and call back the yardage it had in fact traveled. If you were watching this, you'd see Tom swing and call out, for example, "thirty-eight." Mike would shag the ball and call back "thirty-seven," or whatever the number was. The game helped Tom to focus on where he wanted the ball to go, rather than on mechanics or contact. It's one of the reasons Tom was and is so good with his wedges.

Joe Inman told me about a similar game he and his brother used to play when they were kids. The rules were simple. The brothers took turns trying to hit one another with wedge shots from ninety yards and in. If you were the target, you could raise your hands to cover your head. But you couldn't dodge. If the ball hit you in the body, you had to take it.

Those boys learned to focus on their targets.

I'm not saying that you need to find a sibling and start chipping golf balls at his or her solar plexus. But you do need to find a way to get away from standing over the ball worried about what's going to happen.

I had a client once who wanted to try the Champions Tour. His problem was yips with his wedges. I listened to him for a while, and we tried various approaches to improvement. Nothing seemed to work. Finally, I picked up one of the flat boards that separated the hitting stations on the practice range. I tilted it and started rolling balls down the board toward him. He had to hit half wedges while the ball was moving. Immediately, he started hitting deft, crisp pitch shots. The reason was that the moving ball forced him to stop thinking about results and techniques. The novelty and difficulty of hitting a moving ball forced him to think only of the ball. He didn't even have to think of the target.

Defeating putting yips works much the same way. Players with putting yips tend to address the ball seeing and thinking about everything except what they need to focus on. They're worried about the line of the backswing. They're worried about the angle of the putter blade. They're telling themselves not to hit it too hard or too soft and to be sure to release the blade because they've heard that's what Tiger's been working on, even if they don't have the slightest idea of the difference between releasing the putter and releasing a man from jail. They're telling themselves they can't afford to miss this one because it's for par and why couldn't they have hit their previous putt a little closer to the hole and why doesn't the guy they're playing against concede the darned putt?

You've got to clear your mind of all such thoughts. You've got to consistently envision the ball going into the hole, then look at the target, look at the ball, and let the stroke go. You've got to be into the process, not the result. If you follow your mental routine, congratulate yourself. If you don't, try again until you do.

The crux of beating the putting yips is rediscovering the cocky, carefree attitude of a boy who's new to the game and good at it. He believes he's going to make everything he tries.

But if he misses, he doesn't care. He's just a boy, and he's got all the time in the world to get better. If he's twelve, he looks forward to seeing how good he's going to be at thirteen, and he can't even begin to imagine how good he's going to be at sixteen.

You have to think like that kid.

If you have the yips, you can rediscover that confident kid in you. You need more than ever to feed the mind images of the ball going in the hole. I don't care if you have to make some practice putts from a foot to get this process started. Whenever you practice putting, forget mechanics. Think of two things: following your mental routine and seeing lots of balls go in the hole.

Remember that it took you awhile to acquire the yips, and it is likely to take awhile to get rid of them. You are going to have setbacks along the way. You'll miss some four-footers. You'll mishit some pitches. When that happens, you have to be committed to the mental and physical routine you've devised for yourself. If you followed it, be satisfied even if your shot didn't come off as you'd hoped. If you didn't follow it, recommit yourself, beginning with the next shot. The more you can lose yourself in the process and the routine, the more you can be as nonchalant about your putts in competition as you are on the practice green, the easier it is to be consistent and to stack the odds in your favor. You'll start to play well under pressure and love pressure's challenge rather than fear it.

In the fight against the yips, like the fights against all of the other little demons that lurk around the edges of the game of golf, your mind is your ally. See it as a source of strength. Be proud of it. A strong mind is what the heart of a champion is all about.

14.

Confidence and Competence

S ometimes people ask me how much of success in golf is due to the mind and how much is due to the body. Or in a variation of the same thing, they ask how much of golf is a matter of confidence and how much a matter of competence. The honest answer is that I don't know.

Science, including the science of psychology, has not advanced far enough yet to know precisely where the mind ends and the body begins, or vice versa. Nor has it been able to identify, quantify, or even prove the existence of qualities like courage and confidence, qualities that I know exist because I have observed them in champions I've worked with.

So I can't tell you how much better your golf game is going to be if you put the 15th club—confidence—in your bag. Obviously, golf is very much a physical game. If you don't have the physical skills of a professional, it's not likely you're going to be making your living on one of the pro tours until you do.

But I can give you a rough approximation of how much better you can be, given your physical skills, if you have confidence in your game. Take a few golf balls, go to the putting green, and set them down four feet from various holes. Putt half of them as you envision the ball going in. Putt half of them as you imagine the ball rolling past the hole and missing. I'd be very surprised if you don't make more putts thinking about the ball going in the hole than you do thinking about missing.

Or go to the tee on the toughest driving hole on your course, a hole with out-of-bounds down at least one side. Tee up a few balls. Just before you swing at half of them, think about the out-of-bounds stakes. Before you swing at the other half, envision a ball bounding down the middle of the fairway. See which thoughts produce better tee shots.

That's a part of what confidence will do for your game. It will help you see balls going where you want them to go no matter how trying the circumstances. It will help you make your best swings in the clutch.

Consider the case of an actor afflicted with stage fright. In rehearsals, he's the second coming of Marlon Brando. He's got his lines all down. More than that, he's into his character. He puts real emotion into every line. He finds things in the script that the author didn't even know were there, and he makes the audience see them and feel them. But the audience is only the director and a few stagehands. When the curtain rises on opening night, our actor lacks confidence. He might forget a line or two. He's so self-conscious that it gets in the way of the character he's supposed to be playing. His movements are wooden and his words are stilted. He gives a terrible performance.

Is this actor untalented? No, he's not, because his talent is evident at rehearsal. His lack of confidence prevents him from showing what he can do.

Golf can be like that. You've known players who have trouble taking their games from the range to the course. You've perhaps been that player.

The difference is confidence.

Now you know that confidence doesn't have to wait until your swing falls into a groove and you're hitting it the way you want to. You know that confidence is a quality, like stamina, that you can develop if you choose to work on it. You know that you can be a scorer even on days when you're not swinging the club as well as you'd like. You can be a clutch player.

You can do all these things if you make a commitment to a regimen that will build confidence, and then honor that commitment.

You know what you have to do. On a consistent basis, you have to:

- Understand that you own your attitude. You're responsible for it. It's not up to your parents or your coaches or your pro to give it to you. It's up to you. No one can take it away.
- Take pride in your confidence, just as you'd take pride in the strongest part of your game. There is no such thing as being too confident. Cultivate an inner arrogance.
- Monitor your thoughts about golf and stop lying to yourself in the negative.
- Stop seeking perfection. Stop expecting perfection—from yourself or your opponents.
- Reinforce your memory of good shots either by keeping a journal or replaying them in your mind's eye. Feel joy when you hit a good shot, because emotion reinforces memory.

- Let go of the memory of your bad shots. The best way to help you do this is to maintain a cool attitude on the golf course, regardless of the circumstances. Play every shot of your life like it's just you and a friend or family member out on the course in the twilight, hitting a few balls before going home to dinner.
- Visualize the things you want to happen. Set some time aside every day to focus on what you want and picture yourself doing it. Make your visualized experiences as vivid as you possibly can.
- Write affirmations that stress positive aspects about your attitude toward golf and belief in yourself.
- Perceive your golf experiences honestly. If you've made mistakes, learn from them and forget them.
- Be a cheerleader for yourself.
- Give the proper priority to your short game. It is essential to your confidence.

You must understand that this regimen will work only as long as you honor your commitment to it. If you read this book and practice the regimen for a few months, it will help you. But if you then decide, "Okay, I've got it," and stop doing the things that developed your confidence, the game of golf is inevitably going to beat that confidence out of you.

Fortunately, confidence is not like the multiplication tables, which you study in third grade, memorize, and retain for the rest of your life. You need to work to attain confidence. You need to work to maintain it. I say "fortunately" because not all players understand this. Those who do understand it have a competitive advantage.

How much work do you need? It depends on your starting point. If you presently lack confidence, you've got a lot of work to do. Once you've developed some, it might take somewhat less work to maintain it. Some of the professional players I work with prefer to review their attitudes and mental habits during breaks from the Tour. During the golf season, they prefer simply to play. Everyone is different. But just as no one stays fit lying on a couch and watching television, no one stays confident without developing and practicing the habits of mind that build confidence.

Now I'm going to tell you the story of a player who committed himself to just such a regimen—and where it took him.

15.

What I Learned
from Padraig Harrington

Almost a decade ago, my wife, Darlene, got a call from a woman who spoke with a light Irish brogue. The caller was Caroline Harrington, and she wanted to know if her husband, Padraig, could book some time for a session at my home in Virginia. And would we mind if she came along?

Of course, we didn't mind. The visit began a working relationship from which I have learned, I suspect, a lot more than my client. I've learned about mental regimens, about the role of that 15th club, and most of all, about commitment.

I didn't know too much about Padraig when he and Caroline walked through my door. I'd seen his name rising toward the top of the European Order of Merit, but he hadn't won many professional events in Europe at that time. He hadn't placed in the top ten during the few events he'd played in the United States. There hadn't been much written about him on this side of the pond. I was about to learn more.

Padraig grew up in a Dublin district called Rathfarnham. His father, Paddy, in his day, was a famous athlete within Ireland. He played the Irish national sports—Gaelic football and hurling.

When he was done playing, the elder Harrington moved to Dublin and became a member of the national police force, the Garda. He and his wife raised five boys in a three-bedroom house.

Paddy Harrington remained active in sport. He and some colleagues in the Garda founded a golf club, originally for members of the force, called Stackstown. That was where Padraig and his brothers learned to play golf.

Stackstown, Padraig told me, did not have what an American club would consider a proper practice range. There was an empty hillside, perhaps 120 yards long from bottom to top. You could hit a few short irons there to warm up before a round, but no longer clubs. There was no tractor picking up balls and returning them so they could be placed in buckets for those with a yen to beat them. At the top of the hill, there was a practice green with a bunker.

Unbeknownst to Padraig, the facilities were a blessing for a young player. As a boy, he couldn't always get out on the course. But he could and did spend countless hours on and around that practice green. That's more or less the way that Harvey Penick and a lot of wise old golf pros have said kids should learn the game. Figure out how to get the ball in the hole first. The rest can come later.

Padraig figured out how to get the ball in the hole. "There was a stage when I was an amateur," he once told me, "when I couldn't understand why anyone would find the chip shot difficult." His short game was that natural, that instinctive, that finely honed.

When he worked on his full swing, he did it by going out on

the Stackstown course. He would take three or four balls and play them all. It was like playing what in America would be called a scramble. He'd hit several shots, go to the best one, and hit several balls again. Anyone who plays scrambles knows that even four insurance salesmen on an afternoon off can go low in that format. Padraig learned to think that he was capable of going low, even with the swing he had pieced together. He learned to score and to compete, and he began to have success as an amateur. Padraig to this day takes great pride in the fact that he never lost an international amateur match while competing for Ireland.

But his swing didn't impress anyone. Padraig has told me that he can still empathize when he plays a pro-am with partners who quaver over a long iron shot. He used to do that, too.

Neither Padraig nor the people closest to him fully realized the importance of the skills Padraig was developing—knowing the short game, knowing how to manage the golf course, knowing how to score. They thought it was more important to have a fluid, flawless swing. Padraig remembers an uncle who visited the family home around the time Padraig was considering turning pro. "You're not even the best golfer in this house!" the uncle said, suggesting that one of Padraig's brothers had a better swing. And the brother might have.

Padraig was so uncertain of his potential that he enrolled in a night school and studied accounting in the evenings, playing amateur golf during the day. He considered it quite possible that he would make his living as an accountant and limit his golf to amateur events.

He'll tell you that he turned pro, ultimately, because he saw

that amateurs he'd beaten in European competitions were turning pro and making a living at golf. But it's also true that Padraig
is a fiercely competitive person. He generally keeps this side of
his personality in the background, letting the public see his
geniality, his modesty, and his charm—all of which are completely genuine. But he burns to be the best—if not the best in
the world, then the best he can be. He knew he couldn't find out
how good that was if he remained an amateur.

Slowly, a step at a time, he made his way up the ladder of professional golf. Padraig approached his golf career the way an
accountant might approach a commission to audit and restruc-
ture the books of a big new client. He was very systematic. He
took on a fitness coach and lost some weight. Nowadays, you'll
often find him going for a run in the early evening, after a long
day at the golf course. He started working with Bob Torrance on
his swing. They have gradually refined his techniques until
even Padraig's testy old uncle might be impressed by his swing
mechanics.

He began to succeed. He won his first European Tour event
in 1996. The next year he played in his first U.S. Open, at Con-
gressional. He missed the cut and realized his game needed
more work to compete at the highest levels of pro golf. So he
worked harder. In 1998, he played in the Open again, this time
at the Olympic Club in San Francisco. He remembers that week
playing about as well as he thought he could play. He chipped
and putted brilliantly. He finished tied for 32nd.

Some players might have responded to that performance by
relaxing a little. After all, if you finish in the top thirty or so in
the U.S. Open, you can justifiably think of yourself as an estab-

lished professional. Other players, with a different attitude, might have gotten a little discouraged. If you play as well as you possibly can and you finish 32nd, what likelihood is there that you'll ever reach the top?

Padraig's response was neither complacency nor disappointment. He tried to figure out how to get still better. As part of that process, he and Caroline contacted me. As I mentioned, he had already read *Golf Is Not a Game of Perfect*. He told me it had immediately helped him. One of the lessons he drew from it was the importance of not thinking about swing mechanics while playing a competitive round. From that point on, he has almost never done so. Not many players could so abruptly change an old, unhelpful habit. But Padraig is very strong-willed once he's made up his mind to do something.

Padraig instinctively adopted a mental regimen very similar to the one I am presenting in this book. Every year, he reread *Golf Is Not a Game of Perfect*. He made notes from it and he reviewed the notes frequently; these were his affirmations. They changed somewhat over the years as his game evolved and different elements became more important to him. But he made these affirmations part of his regimen.

He also developed a daily habit of visualizing himself playing the sort of golf he wanted ultimately to play. Again, he did this because of what he had read, and because he intuitively realized that he needed a regimen.

I recount this not to advertise *Golf Is Not a Game of Perfect* but to re-emphasize the point that a strong mental game is not something you simply learn. It's something you have to work on consistently and persistently.

Even that did not satisfy Padraig. He wanted to work harder on his mental game, just as he was working on his swing and his fitness. So we began a quest for improvement.

Over the years since then, my role with Padraig has probably involved more listening than talking. Padraig is curious, observant, and analytical. He thinks about what he's done and he learns from his setbacks. Most of the time, when we meet, he'll tell me what's been going on in his game. He'll tell me what he thinks he needs to do to get better. He's usually right. My role becomes nodding, patting him on the back, and saying, "Go get 'em." Padraig rarely needs me to tell him what or how to think. I answer his questions about golf psychology. I affirm his good ideas. I try to nudge him gently back on track when his curiosity leads him in a wrong direction.

Take, for instance the pace at which he plays. Though most Irishmen play a very brisk game of golf, early in his pro career Padraig developed a reputation for slow play. He knew the importance of going through his preshot routine. He knew that he didn't want to swing until his body and his mind were both ready. Sometimes this meant that he took a long time over the ball. Anyone who remembers the 1999 Ryder Cup will probably remember Padraig on the 17th hole of the final Sunday. After hitting his drive, he walked almost all the way to the 17th green, then turned around and walked back down the fairway to his ball. He wanted to be certain he had a clear mental picture of his target.

Anyone who does that on worldwide television will soon hear and read that he's a slow player. And, as the pro tours try to speed the game up a bit, they're beginning to put players suspected of delaying play under a clock. That can disrupt a player's concentration. Amateur players might encounter a similar problem if a course marshal rides up and tells them they've got to play faster.

I've never tried to suggest to a player how fast or how slow his routine ought to be; every player is different. But I do tell them that they need a routine efficient enough that it will keep them from being singled out for time enforcement. They need a routine that will keep their pace of play from ever becoming a distraction. No golfer should ever hit a shot under time pressure, before he feels ready. On the other hand, each golfer should have a routine that gets him ready well before a reasonable allotment of time has expired.

Padraig and I didn't make that a priority until he decided it needed to be. That was after the 2004 Buick Classic at Westchester Country Club. He lost that tournament in a playoff with Sergio Garcia and Rory Sabbatini. He lost it because, just before a crucial shot, he was distracted by some noise or movement in the gallery. He knew instantly that he needed to step away from the ball, clear his mind, and begin his routine again. But he didn't, because he was concerned with his reputation as a slow player. So he hit the shot without a clear mind and a focus on his target. It did not go well, and he lost the playoff to Garcia.

"I knew I should have walked away," he said later.

We decided that he had to compress his routine until he could do it very comfortably in much less time than the rules allow. "You have to have something that will work for you on the 18th green at Augusta or at the U.S. Open," I said. "You have to have something that will work for you in the big moments.

Those are the moments when any little flaw you have will show up."

For Padraig, the solution to the pace of play problem was intensifying his focus on getting into his target. He realized that once he had cleared his mind of all thoughts except thoughts about where he wanted his ball to go, he could simply step up to the shot and go through the physical elements in his routine briskly and efficiently.

But getting into his target was not as easy as it is to write the words. He had to work hard on learning acceptance. Like a lot of golfers, particularly those working to improve themselves, Padraig had a tendency to evaluate and criticize the shots he'd made. "I'm terrible for analyzing," he told me. "I have to really try not to beat myself up."

This is not always a bad tendency to have. There are phases in every good golfer's season and career when training is the highest priority. A player might be trying to refine a part of his swing or his putting stroke or his short game. He's working with a teacher and he's practicing this change. He needs to evaluate, after each practice shot, how well he did. He needs to be sufficiently critical of himself to understand when he fails to execute correctly. He needs to be sufficiently tough with himself to keep working at it until the correct move becomes an ingrained habit.

This training phase might come at the beginning of an amateur's season. For a touring pro, it might come at the outset of a three-week hiatus from competition, when he sets aside entire days to spend on the range, practicing. Jack Nicklaus used to spend time at the beginning of every golf season with the pro who had taught him since boyhood, Jack Grout. They'd look at his swing and reinforce his fundamentals. But once the competitive season began, Nicklaus took lessons from nobody. He understood that the training phase needs to end well before competition starts.

Prior to competition, a player needs to move into the trusting mode, where he has faith in his swing, doesn't try to analyze it, and simply accepts where the ball goes. A player can't shoot his best scores unless he's in the trusting mode. If he's not, he's inevitably going to start thinking about his swing mechanics on the course, and that, in turn, will erode his natural grace, timing, and rhythm. Golfers at their best don't think about their swings; they think about where they want the ball to go. I often counsel players to stay away from tournaments when they're working on swing changes. But given the nature of the tournament schedule and the pressure to improve and compete simultaneously, that's not always easy to do.

Padraig worked for several years to refine his ability to be accepting and therefore to insure that he played competitive golf in the trusting mode. At first, he worked on turning off the critic inside his mind after he'd hit a shot. He reminded himself that he had to accept his results. He reminded himself that he had to stay in the present, and that the shot he'd just hit was in the past. As time went by, he started making acceptance part of his preshot routine rather than something he would do after the shot had been struck. As he visualized the shot he wanted to hit, he would simply know that he'd accept whatever actually happened to the shot.

Someone might object to this notion on the logical grounds that a player cannot be simultaneously visualizing that his golf ball will go where he wants it to go and accepting that it might go somewhere else. I can only reply that great golf minds aren't necessarily logical. Or, perhaps, that our conception of logic isn't sufficiently developed to account for the ways in which the human brain works. All I can tell you for sure is that Padraig, like a lot of great players, could both be absolutely into his target and absolutely certain that he would accept the outcome of the shot, no matter what it turned out to be.

I should add that the ability to accept his shots, especially in competition, was not something that Padraig lacked one day, learned, and then had forever after. The mind of a golfer is rarely that clear-cut. It's more accurate to say that Padraig gradually realized the importance of acceptance and persistently kept trying to acquire it. But, like anyone, he has his bad days as well as his good days. There are times when he relapses and starts analyzing and criticizing himself. Fortunately, he has friends who understand his mind and help him get back on track. One of them is his caddie, Ronan Flood. They're both Dubliners, they're both well educated, and they're in-laws; Ronan married Caroline's sister.

After a round recently, Ronan noticed how Padraig was beating himself up. "Do you think we should iron your hands?" he asked him. It was a reference to a Harry Potter movie they'd both seen. In it, Dobby, the grotesquely self-critical house elf, would punish himself by doing things like taking a hot iron to his hands. Ronan was using the movie and a little humor to make his point.

Padraig laughed. He got it. He still gets it. But acceptance is probably something he's always going to work on. As he has occasionally told me, his problem is not lack of commitment to improvement. It is that he is, if anything, too committed. He is constantly trying to get better. He has a tendency to tinker with things in his game that don't need to be fixed. He has a tendency to be too critical of himself when his performance doesn't meet his expectations.

That's not to say there's no place in the mind of a competitive golfer for analysis and self-criticism. The trick is knowing when and how to apply them. While it's no good to be analyzing and criticizing yourself during competition, it's also important to think back on the results of a competition and learn from them. Padraig does this exceptionally well.

A few years ago, in the Irish Open at Portmarnock, Padraig shot 69 in the first round. It was just the sort of score he likes to shoot in the opening round of a big event. It put him close to, but not in, the lead. It made him feel that he could handle the golf course, but kept him temporarily out of the hot core of the spotlight. It was, he told me later, "a lovely start."

He played that first round in the morning, leaving him a free afternoon. He went to the range and decided to work on making his swing just a little better than it had been in that opening round. And he did. Padraig worked for four hours. Things clicked. He couldn't remember hitting the ball better at any time in his life than he hit it that afternoon on the range at Portmarnock. He wanted to bottle the swing he had during that practice session, to keep it forever. Failing that, he thought, he dearly wanted to hit the ball that well during the second round.

The next day, he got what he was hoping for. He hit the ball magnificently.

He also shot 75 and missed the cut.

Padraig did the wise thing. He didn't try to figure out what was wrong while he was on the course. But afterward, he did. He pondered what had made him go from 69 the first day to 75 the second—with a brilliant swing.

He realized that the four hours he'd spent on the range Thursday afternoon had subtly altered the game he took to the course on Friday. For one, he was so confident in the way he was striking the ball that it affected his judgment and course management. "I took on some shots I shouldn't have taken on because I was hitting it so great," he told me. "I went at some sucker pins." On any golf course set up for a national championship, there are likely to be shots like this. The committee will set pin a few paces away from bunkers, on slopes that insure that if you go into the bunker, you can't get up and down. Or it might set the tees on a short par four up just far enough to tempt players to pull out their drivers and go for the green. The winner in such events is almost always going to be a player who assesses these choices very prudently. He'll be a player who understands when to fire at a flag and when it's better to settle for a twenty-five-foot uphill birdie putt. Padraig normally is such a player. But on that Friday at Portmarnock, he was a gambler. A couple of times, he lost.

He also realized he hadn't putted well in the second round. That puzzled him. He hadn't spent any appreciable time on the putting green the day before. But as he thought about it, he realized that the work he'd done on the range had altered the way he was thinking. He'd shifted his focus from getting the ball to his target to his swing mechanics. That focus didn't automatically shift back just because he was on a putting green in competition. Thinking mechanically, he'd putted poorly.

"Because I had spent four hours thinking about how the club was tracking on the backswing, or whatever the swing thoughts were, when I went to hit a putt the next day, I also had swing thoughts," he later told me. "It was a big eye-opener. By fixing your golf swing during a tournament, it might end up that you chip and putt worse the next day. You can't turn it on and off like a light switch."

Ever since that time, Padraig has tried to avoid tinkering with his swing during tournament weeks. This isn't as easy as it sounds. Swing advice fills the air over the practice tees at tournament sites like the smell of apple pie fills my mother's kitchen. It's hard to resist, especially if you're not hitting the ball the way you'd like. But what Padraig has learned is that scoring well doesn't necessarily mean hitting the ball perfectly. As he found out at that Irish Open at Portmarnock, scoring well depends more on course management and the short game than it does on ball striking.

Let me be clear here. I understand that it's important to hit the ball well. I understand that what Padraig Harrington now considers imperfect ball striking is something that 99.99 percent of the world's golfers would love to have. But if you ask Padraig, he will tell you that he seems to do his best scoring when he feels his swing is a notch below perfect. This forces him to plan each shot carefully and to make prudent choices. He will tell you that in recent years, when he's had his greatest success, he's found himself trying to get back something of what he had when he was just starting out as a pro—that sense of how to score, how to get the ball in the hole despite an imperfect swing, how to work things out when they're not going well.

"I'm a lot better now at shooting 68 than I was then, because I've been working on my technique for ten years," he said recently. "But back then, I used to shoot a lot of 64s and 63s. Of course, I'd match them up with 75s and 74s. Now I have the swing to eliminate the 75s and 74s and I just want to go back to my real talent, which is getting the ball in the hole."

As his mental game has progressed, Padraig has developed what he likes to call a "soft focus" when he plays competitively. It's an example that anyone can learn from. As Padraig begins his preshot routine, his mind is clear. He's thinking about only one thing: his target. But his focus does not cause his jaw to jut or his knuckles to go white. It's not grinding. It's not that intense. Because he already knows that he'll accept whatever happens to his shot, he's relaxed, even serene. He feels as if the most intense part of his routine is picking out his target, deciding where and how he wants the ball to go, and clearing his mind. After that, the actual shot seems of secondary importance.

When he's got that soft focus, Padraig plays his best golf.

As he got better, Padraig had to learn to deal with issues he never dreamed of when he was studying accounting back in Dublin. He's had to learn to be a good interview without letting the media's questions alter his thinking. He's had to learn how to answer questions about Tiger Woods.

For any player, like Padraig, who wants to win major championships, Tiger is like the elephant in the room. He can't be ignored, because once you're contending in major championships, the media won't let you ignore him. They continually ask questions about how you'll cope with him. In fact, I think that one of the many reasons for Tiger's success is that no one ever asks *him* how he's going to handle playing against Tiger. Tiger can focus on his own game.

Padraig quickly figured out that he needed to do the same. A few years ago, he got into contention at the invitational event Tiger sponsors out in California every December. Inevitably, reporters asked him how he was going to handle the pressure of going up against Tiger.

"I'm more concerned about me," Padraig said. "I can't be worried about him. If he plays great, brilliant. But you've got to focus on your own game and not worry about anyone else."

A lot of players say something similar when they're asked about going up against Tiger. Padraig's performances show that his statements are not mere bravado. He truly has learned to play his own game, find his soft focus, and let the results take care of themselves. He beat Tiger in the Target World Challenge in 2002. In 2006, he became only the second player (the other was Billy Mayfair at the Nissan Open in 1998) to best Tiger in a play-off when he won the Dunlop Phoenix in Japan.

That was a memorable event. Both men shot 67 to tie for the title. In the play-off, Padraig drove his ball behind a tree to the left of the fairway. He tried to hit his second shot through a cleft in a tree. It nicked the tree but left him in position to hit a wedge to two feet and make a birdie four that won the hole against Tiger's par five.

Afterward, the press wanted to know how much beating Tiger was going to boost Padraig's confidence. The questions were leading ones, along the lines of, "Now that you've beaten

Tiger, how do you think the confidence from that will affect your chances in the majors?"

Padraig politely told the reporters, in effect, that they had no idea what was going on in his mind. "The fact that I beat him this week doesn't change me as a golfer," he said.

The truth was that Padraig had indeed changed as a golfer in the years since he'd turned pro. But the mere fact that on a play-off hole, he'd made four and Tiger had made five didn't have all that much to do with it. Suppose Tiger had eagled that play-off hole to beat Padraig? Should that have made any difference in Padraig's confidence?

I don't think it would have mattered much to Padraig. He told me not long ago that he had learned the difference between swing confidence and self-confidence. If you've merely got swing confidence, he said, you believe you'll hit the ball well because you have recently been hitting it well. But that confidence disappears quickly when the swing falls out of the groove, as it inevitably will. Self-confidence, to Padraig, was something more valuable. He knew that when he had self-confidence, no matter what circumstances he found himself in, no matter how he was swinging on any given day, he could play his game. His mind would be helping him, rather than hindering him. He judged himself not by whether Tiger made a par or an eagle on a play-off hole, but on how consistently he brought that kind of self-confidence to the course.

Padraig had changed himself, and gained this self-confidence, by years of dedication to improving his body, his swing, and his mind. Together, we had seen milestones that served to mark his progress. The year after he lost to Sergio in that play-off at Westchester, he won the same tournament. He did so by sinking a dramatic ninety-foot putt for an eagle on the final hole. I remember that afterward, he told me that the previous year, he'd had a similar putt. Then, his mind hadn't been clear. He'd thought about getting his aim right and not running it too far past the hole if he missed. But in 2005, he told me, his focus on the target was nearly perfect. "I was just totally into my target and letting whatever happened happen. Going too far or not far enough never crossed my mind. I never worried about my aim or my line. I just saw it and rolled it. When it was six or eight feet from the cup, I knew it was in. But even if it hadn't gone in, I knew that was what I had been looking for. That was where I wanted my head to be."

When I started to hear those kinds of words from Padraig and knew that he was not merely parroting ideas about psychology but was living them, I knew that he was ready to win almost any tournament he entered. Being mentally ready to win does not necessarily mean you will win, especially in a major championship. But it's a huge help.

Padraig had precisely the right attitude after coming up two strokes short and finishing 7th at the 2007 Masters. He told me on Sunday evening that while he hadn't won, he had had played the way he wanted to play. His thoughts had been exactly where they needed to be as he came through the crucible of Sunday afternoon at the Masters. "I know now I can win some of these," he told me, referring to major championships.

I knew that at some point, everything would come together for Padraig. His swing and his mind were already there. He was on the brink of great accomplishments.

16.

Putting It All Together

On the eve of the final round of the 2007 British Open, Padraig Harrington said something I had never heard him say before. We were in the house he'd rented in Carnoustie, a short walk from the golf course. Friends and family had gathered for a quiet party in his support. Padraig at the time lay tied for third, a full six strokes behind Sergio Garcia.

"I hope you've taken Monday off," I heard him tell a friend.

"Why?" the friend asked.

"Because I'm going to win," Padraig said. (The implication was that the friend would be celebrating Sunday night, would miss the flight back to Dublin, and wouldn't be able to get to work on Monday.) At first, Padraig said it in a joking tone. But as he repeated it to me and to others, I could tell that he was trying the idea out, not only on his friends, but on himself.

For these folks, who knew him well, it was a startling statement. Padraig had always been one to shy away from predictions about himself, particularly predictions of victory. As an amateur, if he was talking with a friend before a match, and the friend said, "Well, you should beat so-and-so tomorrow," Padraig would always cut him off.

"Don't say that," he would admonish the friend. Maybe he

thought that predicting victory projected an unseemly arrogance. Maybe he thought that predicting victory would add pressure that he didn't want or need.

But there he was, doing precisely that. He had told me on occasion during the months before the 2007 Open that he finally knew he was capable of winning a major. But he'd never narrowed it down to a specific major, nor to one in which he entered the final round six strokes back.

Under other circumstances, with another player, I might have been worried that someone who started predicting victory on Saturday evening was getting ahead of himself, thinking too much about results, too much about the future. In general, I prefer that players be thinking about the process of playing their best golf, thinking about going through their routines on each and every shot, thinking about letting the results take care of themselves.

But I was not worried about that with Padraig, because I knew how finely he had honed his mental game in preparation for this British Open. I knew he would be focused on all the right things before every shot of Sunday's final round. I knew that he had been working for many years to achieve a state of mind that made it possible for him to play like a champion in the final round of a major. So I was happy to hear him say that he thought he in fact would be the champion.

I couldn't wait to see what was going to happen on Sunday.

I was a houseguest of the Harrington family during Open week. Padraig started inviting me to share the houses he rents during major championships a few years ago. He tells me he's never finished out of the top ten in any tournament where we've shared a house. I'm not sure there's a cause-and-effect relationship there. But I like the arrangement because it gives me a bed close to the golf course, where I work during the day with many clients. It gives me a chance to talk casually with Padraig in the evenings.

During this Open week, I felt I needed to make a contribution. The only tangible effect I'd had on Team Harrington prior to the tournament was to deny bed rest to Padraig's caddie, Ronan Flood. Ronan and I were supposed to share a bedroom. I have to confess that my snoring had driven Ronan to the couch in the living room.

I did, in return for my bed and board, give Padraig and Caroline an occasional assist with their son, Paddy. Paddy was, at the time, a lively three-year-old. Like any three-year-old, he can't get enough of his parents' attention, particularly his dad's. I wanted to make sure Padraig had time during the evening to think about golf and to visualize the results he wanted. So I played with Paddy. For a few nights, I'd pretend that Paddy was a magician or wizard. He'd take a stone from behind the fireplace and put it in one hand or the other, behind his back. I'd try to guess which hand the stone was in. Once I'd guessed, he would switch the stone to the hand I hadn't guessed. Once again, the clever young wizard would trick the sports psychologist. But by Saturday night, I guess Paddy was bored with tricking me. He needed something new. So I taught Paddy an old trick I'd learned as a kid in Vermont, called Skin the Cat. I'd straddle him, take him by his hands, and let him turn a flip. He was just the right age and size for it. If we'd let him, he would gladly have stayed up past midnight, skinning a couple of million cats. He loved it. And while Paddy skinned cats, his father was able to focus calmly on the golf tournament. He did his visualization exercise and went to sleep.

There was not much I could contribute in the way of advice to Padraig. He'd taken care of nearly all the preparation himself. In addition to his faithful commitment to his mental game regimen, Padraig had made smart choices about getting ready for this particular Open. During the week before the Open, most players either went somewhere to practice or played in the Scottish Open at Loch Lomond, outside of Glasgow. Loch Lomond is a fine course, but it's an inland, parkland style layout. Padraig chose to play (and win) an event with a small purse, the Irish PGA. It was held at the European Club, on the coast of the Irish Sea, about fifty miles south of Dublin. The European Club has a challenging links course, so Padraig was acclimating himself to the wind and terrain he would encounter at Carnoustie. More important, he was protecting himself from the urge to tinker with his swing, an urge that can be very seductive and hard for a golfer to resist if he's standing on a practice tee, hitting ball after ball the week before a big event. The time I worry most about Padraig is when he's got a couple of weeks on a practice tee. His decision to play in the Irish PGA not only prepped him well for Carnoustie. It kept his mind securely in the trusting mode.

When we chatted at night, I heard nothing to suggest that his mind wasn't exactly where it needed to be. I remember one conversation where he told me that he was putting just as he wanted to do it. "I putt my best when I have no awareness of aiming my putter face and no awareness of how hard to hit it, when I'm just into my target. But I'm not concerned about a result, and it's a very soft focus, rather than a hard focus. And that's the way I'm putting now."

I could only nod and tell him to keep thinking that way. People might imagine that there's some sort of special advice a sports psychologist saves to give to a player on the eve of a major championship. There isn't. I might tell a player as he prepares for a major that he needs to anticipate a few different situations he will encounter, from the speed of the greens to the crush of the media. He needs to be mentally prepared for the special difficulties presented by things like the depth of U.S. Open rough. But apart from that sort of adjustment, there isn't anything I tell a player before a major that I wouldn't tell my dad on the night before the finals of member-guest at the Rutland Country Club in Vermont.

On that Saturday evening in Carnoustie, we talked a little bit about the position Padraig was in. You never want to be six shots back, but if ever there was a time and place when six shots wasn't a big lead, it was Carnoustie in 2007. There was only one other player between Padraig and Sergio, so Padraig wouldn't have to pass a lot of people. The course, as Jean Van de Velde can tell you, could make a big lead disappear very quickly.

On the other hand, we agreed, there was nothing Padraig could do about Sergio or anyone else. The only player he could affect was himself. So he had to concentrate on himself and not worry about what anyone else was doing. That's a cliché in golf, but it's no less true for being so.

I reminded Padraig of the way he'd felt on Sunday evening at

Augusta three months before. He'd finished 7th in the Masters that day, but he'd come off the course happy with the way he'd played, happy with where his mind had been all week.

"I want you to have that same feeling when you walk off the course tomorrow evening, whether you're *the* winner or just *a* winner," I said. It was a distinction we'd discussed before. Every golf tournament has a winner, of course. No player has complete control of who that winner will be. Sometimes, someone else will get a break or just play better. But a player can control whether he plays like a winner, whether he masters himself and his mind, whether he thinks appropriately all the way around the golf course. That's not easy to do when you're tantalizingly close to a goal you've pursued for much of your life. A player who can do it is *a* winner, even if it turns out that he's not *the* winner.

I did not discuss much of Padraig's strategy and game plan with him. He mentioned that he was going to change one thing for the final round. On good links courses, where the design makes the player confront the wind coming from every direction of the compass, there's a tendency to try to work the ball both ways. The player tries to draw the ball when the wind is quartering from the left, to hold it against that wind. He tries to cut the ball when the wind is coming from the opposite side. It's an elegant way to play when it works. But it can backfire, either because the player starts to think too much about his swing mechanics or because he hasn't got the sort of swing that lends itself to working the ball both ways. Some players have a natural draw and some have a natural fade. Although any pro who plays into contention in a major can probably hit it both ways on the range, it can be advisable to stick with your natural shot under extreme pressure. That's what Padraig told me he was going to do. He was going to stick with his natural shot, a draw, all the way around on Sunday. That sounded wise to me.

We didn't discuss strategy for each hole. I want a player to have a game plan. But I knew Padraig and Ronan had been working on that plan throughout their practice rounds. I knew that they'd thought through the different ways Padraig might play each hole, depending on the wind and the weather, on hole locations, on his standing in the tournament. On top of that, they knew the course much better than I did. I'd never seen Carnoustie before that week. Padraig had played it many times, beginning in his amateur days. Even if the tournament had been on my home course in Virginia, though, I wouldn't have tried to suggest strategy to Padraig. A player's strategy must depend on a lot of factors that only he can evaluate. Some holes, for instance, look inviting to certain players. Maybe they like downhill tee shots or uphill tee shots or left-to-right doglegs or right-to-left doglegs. Maybe strategy on a hole is affected by a slightly more subtle factor, like a distant bunker that provides an unreachable target for a tee shot or the way trees frame a particular green. Whatever the reason, a player needs to trust his own instincts. He needs to take them into account when he formulates his game plan. Only he really knows what they're telling him.

I had, earlier in the week, talked with Padraig a little bit about the 18th hole. In the years since Jean Van de Velde lost the Open there in 1999, I've been asked many times what I thought about the decisions he made. I've always said that I couldn't second-guess any player in that situation. I would only hope that the player was following a plan he'd made beforehand, not making impulsive decisions. After I saw the 18th for myself, I was still more convinced that there was no particularly safe way to play it. It's the toughest closing hole I've ever seen on a major championship golf course. During the practice rounds prior to the tournament, I saw lots of players make sixes and sevens there. Augusta National's 18th is a tough driving hole. But it's not a hard hole for a professional to make a five on. It was easy to go well beyond five on number 18 at Carnoustie.

Van de Velde had been criticized for hitting a driver off the tee in 1999. But a player who took an iron for his tee shot brought into play trouble that a driver might carry. And no matter what club a player chose, he still had to deal with the Barrie Burn twice and avoid the out-of-bounds line to the left of the green. It's just a terribly difficult hole. I told more than one person that by the time the 2007 Open was over, Jean Van de Velde would very likely be looking a whole lot better, because lots of people were going to make sixes and sevens on the 18th.

Padraig had to deal with his own history on 18. He'd lost a British Amateur he might have won there because of a drive out of bounds. Of course, I didn't recall that history with him. There was no point in belaboring it. He knew that he had to play his shots on 18 in the same frame of mind he needed for every other hole on the course. I simply noted that he and Ronan needed to have a plan for any of the contingencies they were likely to face when they walked onto the 18th tee. They did, and that was all we said about it. Padraig, I felt, had put the problems he'd had on the 18th behind him. He told me he felt he had more experience on Carnoustie than anyone else in the field. He reckoned that to be an advantage. He knew how to play it.

Looking back, there were a couple of things I said and did that might have helped Padraig that evening before the final round. At one point in our conversation, Padraig started talking about some new insights he was having into the mental game. He'd started to ponder the different roles his subconscious and conscious minds play. He wanted to talk about ways that he could strengthen his subconscious self-image, just as I suggested that you do earlier in this book. That's one of Padraig's best characteristics. He's never satisfied with himself. He's always looking for ways to improve.

But there are times and places for doing that sort of fundamental work on the psyche, and the night before the final round of a major championship is not one of them. "I think you're in a great place right now," I said to him. "We'll talk about that another time." And I am sure we will.

On Sunday, Padraig got off to a start much like the ones he'd envisioned the night before. He made three birdies and no bogeys on the front nine. He told me later that he felt that he was just playing the game, hitting the shots. He had no sensation of trying hard. He was playing the final round of the British Open. But mentally, he could have been wandering the course at Stackstown on a summer evening, hitting three or four balls, playing a scramble with himself.

Garcia, by contrast, made three bogeys against one birdie. When Sergio bogeyed the 8th and Padraig birdied the 9th, the lead that had seemed so huge the night before was down to a single, very slender stroke.

Maybe the only person in Scotland who didn't know this was

Padraig Harrington. Padraig doesn't watch scoreboards. He relies on Ronan to do that for him. He sometimes gets a sense of where he stands by the way crowds form and the way they cheer. Sometimes he gets a hint by the club or the line Ronan recommends for a particular shot. But he doesn't want to break his focus on his targets by looking at scoreboards and starting to think about their implications.

Padraig certainly knew he was playing well after he birdied the 11th hole to go four under for the day. He could guess from the gallery that he was getting closer. But he had no idea what Garcia was doing and no idea how close the tournament had become until Ronan handed him his 5-wood on the 14th tee. The 14th is a par five that's reachable in certain winds, but there are some pot bunkers in the area where a driver might land. Padraig and Ronan had agreed that he'd risk the driver on 14 only if he was well off the lead and needed to gamble on making an eagle three. When Ronan handed him the 5-wood, Padraig realized he must be close. (He was in fact tied for the lead at that moment.) Padraig didn't ask Ronan what the leaderboard looked like, and Ronan didn't tell him. But Padraig felt a rush of adrenaline, knowing the game was on. As it happened, Padraig pushed his tee shot slightly and the ball stopped just a yard or two shy of those pot bunkers, vindicating his and Ronan's strategy. Then he hit a fantastic second shot and made eagle anyway.

That put him temporarily into the lead at nine under par. Sergio battled back with birdies at 13 and 14 to square the tournament. But Padraig was oblivious to that. He made his pars on the next three holes.

I watched all this from off the golf course, first in the players' dining room and later in one of the corporate tents overlooking the 18th fairway. It's odd what sticks in your mind from an afternoon like that. I remember in the players' dining room someone commented on the brisk way that Padraig was playing. "He just gets up there and rips it," the player said.

I remembered the work Padraig had done to compress his routine, to make it a routine that would work for him under the most intense pressure. This was certainly such an occasion, and his improved routine was serving him well.

Padraig came to the 18th at nine under par. Sergio had bogeyed the 15th to fall back to eight under. Playing ahead of Padraig, Argentinian Andres Romero had run off four consecutive birdies, getting it to nine under before making six at the 17th and five at the 18th to fall back to six under. But Padraig, thanks to paying no attention to the leaderboards, had no idea what Romero was doing. His only idea was to par number 18.

Ronan handed Padraig the driver. This was the right club, because it was the club they'd planned to play if they got to 18 within a shot of the lead either way. If you're in that situation, you have to play to make four or even three. You have to assume that the players close to you will par the hole. If Padraig's lead had been two strokes or three, Ronan would have suggested a different club. But it was a one-shot lead, and they were executing their plan for that contingency. Padraig's job was merely to put the tournament situation, his boyhood dreams, and all of the hole's trouble out of his mind. He had to pick a target for his tee shot and go through his routine.

He didn't quite manage it. As he told me later, he was playing into a right-to-left wind. He'd been relying on his natural draw all day, but he didn't want to risk drawing the ball, having the wind turn the draw into a hook, and seeing his ball bounce out of bounds. So he decided to hit a slight fade, holding the ball against the wind, making it go dead straight down the fairway. He wanted to hit the shot with a neutral clubface. This means that the clubface would be exactly perpendicular to his intended line, and the slight fade would come from a minutely outside-to-in swing plane. But as he waggled, he looked down at his club-face and it seemed to him that he had inadvertently "strengthened" it. In other words, his clubface was angled slightly to the left.

Padraig told me later that he should have stopped and regrouped. He didn't. As he started to swing, he thought the strengthened clubface might produce a draw, the opposite of what he wanted. He tried to avert this in midswing, and he overcompensated. The result was a tee shot blocked to the right, into the Barrie Burn.

It goes to show two things. One is that no matter what level of golf you're playing, you must strive to clear your mind of conflicting thoughts before you swing. You need a single, clear picture of where you want the ball to go and how you're going to make it go there. If you don't have that single, sharp picture, stop your routine and get it before you proceed.

The second is that even champions sometimes fall short of this standard. Very few players manage to have their minds exactly right for every shot during a casual round, let alone a major championship.

Not only did Padraig lose a penalty stroke when he dropped a new ball at the edge of the hazard, but he was left with a terribly difficult second shot. He was 229 yards from the hole. He still had the right-to-left wind to deal with. The burn wound its way in front of the green. And there were out-of-bounds markers just to the left of the green. He decided to try again to hold the ball against the wind by hitting a cut, meaning he had to aim at the out-of-bounds markers. Just the sort of shot you'd like to hit on the 72nd hole of a major championship you'd been dreaming of winning all of your life, with one ball already in the burn, with a worldwide television audience watching, with the specter of Jean Van de Velde seeking to worm its way into your mind.

It was, he told me later, a shot he might not have attempted in other circumstances. At another time, he might have decided to lay it up short of the burn with his third shot, pitch on, and try to get away with a five by making a putt. But he didn't feel that he had that option, given the circumstances. So he went for the green, but hit the ball a trifle fat and put it in the burn for the second time. Padraig told me later that as the second ball disappeared into the water, he couldn't keep thoughts of Van de Velde out of his mind. He knew he needed to get the ball up and down to at least better the seven Van de Velde had made in 1999. And the next shot, his fifth, was not an easy one. He would have to hit a precisely controlled forty-seven-yard wedge from a tight lie, over water.

I was watching this from a corporate tent alongside an old friend and client, David Frost. We saw Padraig take his drop and begin making practice swings. From a distance, they looked like full swings. "Oh, my God, those are big swings," David said.

I saw it differently. I had seen those sorts of swings before. I could see that his head was up. His body language looked positive. From somewhere, he had summoned the nerve to get back into his routine. "That's the way Padraig does it," I told David.

"They look too big to me," David said.

They weren't. Padraig later told me that he thought acceptance and routine had saved him. He put the two failed shots out of his mind. He put the situation out of his mind. His thoughts as he prepared for the shot were not that he had to get the ball up and down to give himself a chance. They were not about the tournament or the situation. "Right," he told himself. "Let's go through it." And he did. He saw the shot he wanted. He cleared his mind of everything but that soft focus on the target.

He hit a lovely wedge that landed just beyond the pin. It seemed to want to spin back to tap-in range, but for some reason, it didn't. He was left with a testing four-foot putt, but he rolled it right into the center of the cup.

Padraig had fallen from first to second. For a moment, he told me later, he felt disappointed. But only for a moment. Caroline released Paddy, who ran onto the green to be swept up into his father's arms. As far as Paddy was concerned, his dad was the champion. It was not something Padraig and Caroline had planned. But there is something to be said for seeing the world, if only for a moment, through the eyes of a child. It was a reminder that there are more important things in life than who finishes first in a golf tournament, even the British Open. I thought it was a beautiful thing to see.

By the time Padraig stepped off the green, still carrying little Paddy, smiling, waving to the crowd with his free arm, he had recovered his equilibrium. He knew the tournament was far from over. Sergio had a one-stroke lead, but he still had to play 18. I figured there was maybe a one percent chance Sergio would par the hole. It's that tough.

I hurried through the crowd to the scorer's trailer. I wanted to speak to Padraig when he emerged from it. When he did, I caught his eye. "That was the greatest up-and-down I ever saw in my life," I told him.

We walked over to the practice green. I had seen Sergio hit his second shot left of the green, into a bunker. There was no need to watch him try to get the ball up and down to win the tournament. The noise of the crowd would tell us what happened. We did not hear the roar that would have erupted if Sergio had made his par putt. Nor did reporters rush Padraig on the practice green, which they would have done if Sergio had made six. So we knew that Sergio had made a bogey, meaning that he and Padraig had tied for the championship. There would be a four-hole play-off to determine the winner.

Padraig wanted to hit a few putts to keep loose while he waited. But little Paddy was by now a very wired three-year-old. His body was pumping enough adrenaline to fuel a combat regiment. Every time Padraig tried to hit a putt, little Paddy ran up to the ball and kicked it like a soccer ball, off the green. He did this four or five times, laughing merrily, having a grand time. At first, it was funny to watch. But Padraig really needed to hit a few putts to help him get his mind back into golf. Somehow, we had to divert little Paddy's attention in a way that wouldn't get him upset.

"Come on, Paddy," I said. "Let's skin the cat."

So that's one way I helped Padraig Harrington get ready for the British Open play-off. I played Skin the Cat with his son on the putting green. Padraig managed to roll a few practice putts. Eventually, Caroline made her way through the crowd and took Paddy off my hands. I had a chance to talk to Padraig just before the play-off started.

"I think maybe Paddy was trying to tell us something," I said.

"What's that?" Padraig asked.

"He's trying to tell us it's just a game. He doesn't know it's the British Open or what it means. He just thinks it's a game, and he's having fun. Let's learn from that. Let's play the game."

Padraig nodded.

"If you ever wanted to know if you had the ability to hit your absolute best shot under the greatest conceivable pressure," I said, "you just found out with that pitch shot on 18."

We started walking toward the first tee.

"All week long, you've just been into your target and into acceptance," I said. "Let's forget about Sergio. Let's forget about everything but being into the process and doing your routine on every shot. Let's love it. This is where you want to be. Let's have a ball."

Padraig looked at me and said something that amazed me then and amazes me still.

"When you see me waving to the gallery, you and I will be the only two who know that I'm not really waving to the gallery. I'm holding the Claret Jug to the sky. That's the way I visualized it last night."

As I've said, Padraig had never, until the night before the final round, been one to predict that he'd win. He'd always been the opposite. He might say that his goal was to do his best on every shot, to be into his target. But he'd never told me he'd foreseen himself hoisting a trophy.

I could have been concerned that Padraig was letting his mind slip out of the present and into the future. That can be disastrous for a golfer. If you still have golf left to play, you can't be thinking about how you'll spend the money you're going to take from your buddies or whether bogey on the last hole will mean you break 90 or whom you'll thank in your trophy acceptance speech. But there's a subtle difference between that kind of dangerous forward thinking and what Padraig was saying to me. He wasn't composing an acceptance speech. He was just expressing confidence that he was going to win.

"That's great," I said. "Go get 'em."

He strode toward the first tee. I felt good about his chances. So did he, he told me later. He thought that he would be into his process throughout the play-off. He didn't know whether Sergio would be or not. He felt that he had the advantage.

I have always told players that they need to play more aggressively in play-offs than they do under normal tournament circumstances. That's especially true in the PGA Tour's sudden death play-offs. The people you're competing against are excellent players at the top of their games, or they wouldn't have tied for the championship. You can't play conservatively and wait for them to make mistakes. They probably won't. There's a little more room for caution in the four-hole play-off format the British Open uses. But you still have to play with your foot on the gas, not the brake.

Padraig did precisely that on the first play-off hole. Sergio missed the green, hitting his approach into a difficult bunker. Seeing that happen to a play-off opponent, a lot of players would have aimed well away from the hole, which was tucked on the right side, guarded by another bunker. They would have tried to make par, hoping that Sergio would not get his ball up and down, so they'd take a one-stroke lead. Padraig was having none of that. He ripped a 7-iron right at the flag. His boldness was rewarded when he birdied the hole and Sergio made five. He had a two-shot lead.

A two-stroke lead in a four-hole playoff is fine to have, but Padraig was by no means home. Sergio hit the pin on the long par-three 16th. Padraig hit a good shot that rolled off the green. Both players were showing their mettle. Sergio's birdie putt just missed. Padraig rolled his ball through the close-cropped fringe to within three feet and made his par putt. It was a reminder of how narrow the margin between winning and losing can be at the highest levels of golf. Had Sergio's ball fallen in the hole for an ace, or dropped within tap-in range for a birdie—both possible results on that hole—the play-off could have ended differently. Padraig's performance would not have changed, but the outcome might have.

At 17, Padraig hit a beautiful approach shot to eight or ten feet. But, as he later told me, he did not get a clear picture of the target in his mind before he hit his birdie putt. At the last second, he decided to play a little less break. He told me he should have backed away. But he did not, and he missed the putt. Again, it showed that even a great player, in the midst of winning a major, is not always flawless. The most important thing was that Padraig was still accepting whatever happened. As soon as that flawed stroke was done, he put it out of his mind and focused on the next one.

He still had that two-shot lead as he stepped onto the 18th tee for the second time that afternoon. Once again, Ronan handed him the club that corresponded to their plan. With a two-stroke lead, Padraig could afford to play for a five. Ronan handed him a hybrid iron. Padraig put the ball in the fairway. Even then, the tournament was not his. I remember watching him prepare to hit the second shot at 18, trying to leave himself a comfortable wedge into the green for his third. The landing area for that layup shot had looked as narrow as a New York alley when I walked the course. But Padraig found it. The wedge he hit into the green was not as good as the one he'd hit to save the tournament on the 72nd hole. He later told me he pulled it a bit.

Padraig had a thirty-foot par putt. Sergio had a slightly shorter birdie putt. Padraig wanted to make his, to shut the door. He envisioned the ball trickling into the hole, and he was amazed when it rushed past and went three or four feet beyond it. A few moments later, Sergio rolled his birdie putt five feet past. Maybe the green was deceptively quick. Maybe they were both a little pumped. Whatever the reason, they both left themselves testing putts.

Sergio went first and rolled his in from five feet. I watched carefully to see if Padraig was following at least the physical aspects of his routine. He was. He later told me that he was into his routine mentally as well. He didn't think about the situation. He didn't think about what sinking the putt would mean. He didn't think about the mechanics of his stroke. There was only the ball and the hole. Padraig rolled it into the middle of the cup.

A few moments later, Peter Dawson, secretary of the Royal and Ancient, pronounced Padraig Harrington the champion golfer of the year. Padraig raised his hand to the sky. This time the Claret Jug was really in it.

Neither Padraig nor I are much for drinking, but we had a few that night. Padraig was surrounded by old friends. Just as he'd predicted, they missed their flights back to Dublin and needed to take Monday off. No one cared. Many of them told me that they'd played against Padraig when he was a kid. They'd thought back then that he was a great guy. But none of them had ever thought he'd be a great player. They were proud and happy, so happy that they almost felt they'd won the British Open themselves. They knew how much work he had done to become a major champion.

I was also thinking about all the work he'd done, about the way he'd faithfully stuck to his mental regimen, year after year. It had not made him perfect, of course. But when he'd needed it most, after hitting two balls in the water on the 72nd hole, his work had paid off. He was able to accept what had happened, to put it out of his mind, and to focus on the shot at hand. We talked a little bit about that moment.

"You just knew you were going to get it up and down to win," I said.

"There was a time when I would've convinced myself that I had blown the tournament," he replied. "I would've been down and discouraged. But today it never entered my mind."

I could not have been prouder of him than I was at that moment.

I have often thought, since that day, about what Padraig said to me on the practice green before the play-off—that when he raised his hand and waved to the crowd, he would, in his mind, be holding the Claret Jug. I've thought about his uncharacteristic prediction on the eve of the final round that he would be the Open champion.

Of course, if winning tournaments were as simple as predicting you would win, everyone would do it. It's not that simple. Bravado doesn't win tournaments. Nor is it as simple as truly believing you'll win. If it were, hypnotists would have a thriving business convincing golfers they were about to win major championships.

What happened to Padraig was the spontaneous culmination of years of effort. He reached the point where he was not only comfortable with his own ability under pressure. He was comfortable talking about it with other people.

This doesn't mean that if Padraig believes and predicts he's going to win his next major it will automatically happen. It won't. Other contestants will, on other days, play better than he does. Their balls will bounce the right way and their putts will drop. He won't be able to control that.

It does mean that when Padraig feels this way, he will play without doubt and fear. He will play as well as he can. He will play like a winner, even if he isn't the winner on that particular day.

Not many players get to that point, because not many are

willing to do the work Padraig did. It began with all those boy-hood hours around the practice green at Stackstown. It continued through all the hard work he did with Bob Torrance on his swing and the equally difficult work he did with me on his mind. That's a huge commitment, a commitment that requires more time than most amateur golfers have.

But if you're a golfer who wants to play better, to see what it means to play your best golf, there is much you can learn from Padraig Harrington. You, too, can follow a mental regimen. You, too, can discipline your mind. You, too, can know that in the most important rounds of your life, you'll play without doubt and fear. You can know that you'll play with a 15th club, that you'll play like a winner.

When you do that, you might be surprised at how often you'll also be *the* winner.

Affirmations

Some of the golfers who read my books want more. They tell me they learned from what they read. Their games improved. But they need additional material, material specifically for them.

"Can you tell me exactly what to do?" they ask. "Can you write out a program I can do every day?"

It's not quite that simple. No two golfers are alike. Their mental issues are distinctly their own. The time they have to devote to golf varies. So does their willingness to devote a significant chunk of that time to getting better. I've had clients who tell me they'll spend whatever time it takes to reach their goal of getting to scratch or playing on the elite amateur level or making it big on the PGA Tour. Other clients tell me that their first priorities have to be family and career. They know, more or less, the amount of time and effort that would be required to move from, say, a six handicap to scratch. They simply can't justify the expenditure of that time. But they'd still like to think that when they can get away for a round of golf, their mental game will be an asset rather than a handicap. I can understand their decision. It's fine with me.

Whichever sort of golfer you are, you need to come up with your own mental regimen, one that's appropriate for you and you alone. It must respond to your unique golf game and your particular mental strengths and weaknesses. It must be something you can commit yourself to, given the particular circumstances and time constraints of your life.

In this appendix, I will guide you by offering suggestions and examples. The first step is to come up with a set of affirmations that you will read several times a day or as often as possible. As I told you earlier in this book, affirmations are thoughts that you choose for yourself. Just as protein is required to build muscle, affirmative thoughts are required to build a strong subconscious self-image. Writing down affirmations for yourself and reviewing them regularly do for your mind what drinking protein shakes does for your body.

Your affirmations must be personal, yours alone. I can't give you those. What I can do is give you generic affirmations. Each of them covers a specific area of the game. Some golfers may need to cover only one or two of those areas. Some may need all of them. You have to decide which ones are appropriate for you.

Don't photocopy these generic affirmations or carry this book around like a prayer book you read each day. Use my affirmations as guides to write your own. Then put your affirmations in a plastic sleeve or on your computer desktop or someplace where they'll be secure and readily available.

Write them in the present tense, as if you have already accomplished your goal.

Keep them positive. Say what you want to accomplish, not what you're trying to avoid.

Read your affirmations several times a day if you can. As you read, try to visualize yourself performing well. Try to feel the environment of a golf course or a tournament. Attach emotions to your reading. Do it slowly. If you rush the experience, it won't be as helpful.

Sustain the commitment to your affirmations until you automatically and naturally, without prompting, see yourself as the golfer you've written about. Sustain it until you have a new habit and belief system, until your subconscious self-image has permanently changed for the better. The amount of time this will take varies with each individual.

Winning

I am a winner. I love the feeling of coming down the stretch in the lead, tied for the lead, or near the lead. Being here is why I practice and play in competition. I am cool and calm. I love knowing that I will do my routine with a clear mind on every shot. I am committed to my target on every shot. Nothing bothers me or upsets me.

Total acceptance is my motto. I can accept whatever happens because I know I have controlled what I can control, my mind. I know I will play my game and win the battle with myself.

I live in the present moment. Any time I even begin to get ahead and think about winning or losing, I catch the thought and throw it away. I get back to my next shot.

I am at peace on the course because I assume I will win before the tournament and the round starts. I am into my game. I never care about scoreboards or what others are doing because I love and trust my own game.

Putting

I am a great putter. I always make putts when they matter the most. But I am great because I treat all of my putts the same. I give every putt the same low level of importance.

I have a great instinct for effortlessly reading greens. I trust my reads, commit to them. Then I get into my target and execute my routine on every shot. Nothing tempts me away from this process. Results have no impact on me because I just want to make every putt in my mind.

I am playful when it is time to putt. I am very visual on the greens, and I love envisioning the ball go in the hole.

I am positive and patient. I love to putt. The putting green is where the real game begins. I own the putting green. It is my favorite place. It is where I have an edge. It's where I separate myself from others.

Driving

I am a pure ball striker off the tee. I love to show off my driving skills in tournaments and on challenging driving holes. Others always tell me how well I drive the ball. I simply see myself hitting good drives.

If I occasionally miss a fairway, it means nothing to me. I never carry a miss over to my next shot. I see my shot, see my target, and let it happen.

I feel that driving the ball is a great strength that gives me an edge. My eyes and my mind are always locked into my target. My eyes never wander and my mind never wavers. I feel like I have a laser beam between my eyes that goes to my target and I never leave the beam.

My mind is clear. My swing feels effortless. The ball feels light on my clubface. Driving feels automatic. I feel so confident I hit driver most of the time on par fours and par fives. The exceptions are when my length would cause me to run out of fairway. What is right or left of the fairway is never a concern to me. I see only my target.

Pitching

I love to hit pitch shots. I see it and do it. The ball goes where I'm looking, with the trajectory I envision and with the sound, feel, and spin I expect. I feel that pitching the ball is easy and predictable. I love to show off my pitching in competition. Thin lies or hardpan lies are my favorites, but the lie means little to me. Wherever the ball lies, I know I will see the shot and react to my target.

I feel that I hit these shots with my eyes and my instincts. I know when I do this I have a smooth, athletic rhythm and a languid flow.

When I practice, I pretend I'm at my next tournament. When I'm in a tournament, I pretend I'm at home in my favorite practice area.

Pitching seems so simple. I know if I am into my process, rather than results, it will just happen. It's like an out-of-body experience where I step outside myself and pitch the ball unconsciously.

I love to hole shots with my pitches. I never worry about getting the ball up and down. This is my edge.

Going Low

I shoot a lot of low numbers because numbers mean nothing to me. They're just pencil marks on a scorecard. There are no limits unless we make them up. There are no limits because a limit implies that there is perfection, a point no one can attain. There is no such thing as perfect in golf. I never make up limits.

I just relish seeing how low I can keep going, breaking through imaginary belief barriers that seem to hold others back.

I love making birdies more than I hate making bogeys. I love going low more than I hate shooting over par. I love one-putting more than I hate three-putting. I love pitching in more than I hate not getting the ball up and down. I live to win, to go low, to hold course records. I love to win big. I know my attitude and lack of fear amaze others. That makes it even more fun. But I find playing golf free of belief barriers, fear, and doubt gratifying in itself.

Emotional Maturity

I pride myself in being a consistent and steady golfer in competition. Nothing ever bothers me or fazes me. I am like granite. I am solid. To galleries and my fellow competitors, I am as calm as still water in a deep pool. They know that nothing will ever upset me. I am imperturbable.

Resilience is my middle name. I always hang in there during adversity. I stay patient, looking for something good to happen. I know it will if I am patient long enough. I know I will be patient longer than anyone else.

I never let myself get frustrated, try to force things, or try to make anything happen. It's amazing how often I wait and wait, then birdie three of the last four holes to keep myself in a tournament or record a great score.

I take great pride in this emotional maturity and patience because no one gave me this attitude. I developed it. I gave it to myself. I earned it. It is now one of my most valued strengths.

Practicing the Short Game

I pride myself for investing quality practice time in the short-game area every day. It's not a chore. I love to practice pitching, bunker play, and putting. I love it when others are on the range hitting balls and I'm in the short-game area, because I know this is where I will separate myself from others in tournament play. I'm in the short-game area first every day. I practice there when

I'm fresh, because I recognize the short game's importance. I never forget this. It's my bread and butter, my pride and joy.

I sustain my commitment to the short game and the scoring clubs because I am dedicated to seeing how good I can get at golf. Practicing short-game shots regularly, with quality and focus, is a key to the quest and a critical part of the process.

Mental Preparation

I take tremendous pride in how thoroughly I prepare my mind before every competitive round I play. I take twenty to thirty minutes of quiet time to go over the next day's round in my mind. I prepare to think of nothing but my target when I stand over every shot. I will be into the target as a process with no concern for the result. I will have a clear and focused mind. Long before traveling to the golf course, I will know where my mind will be for every shot.

I will be committed and decisive. I will be patient. I will live in the present moment and play one shot at a time until I run out of holes. I will play my game and have no concern for or interest in anything anyone else is doing. I will respect and trust my game.

It is so much fun to play this way, knowing I have done all my mental and physical preparation. My game plan is laid out. I know my target. All that's left is to go out and execute.

Adversity

I am strong, and I take great pride in that strength. I thrive by turning adversity into more strength. The struggle makes me stronger. When the game knocks me down, I always want to stand a little taller when I get back up.

I love golf in part because it does sometimes knock me down and make me stand taller. If I love golf only when everything is going my way, I don't really love the game.

When I struggle, it can at times feel as if I have no game at all, as if my entire game stinks. But I know this is false. I must keep my views in perspective. Things are never as bad as they sometimes seem. What really matters is not the situation but how I respond to the situation.

I can't change the past, but I can change the future. I will learn whatever is useful to know from my recent poor performance. I will forget the rest and go forward with confidence.

I just didn't play like myself. That wasn't the real me out there. I haven't lost the ability to play great golf. I just need to get back to thinking well and playing with a clear mind.

I must stop feeling sorry for myself, stop wallowing in self-pity. I must pick myself up, hitch up my pants, and start turning myself around. It's gut-check time. I face a challenge, a test. And I love it. Right now, I can either sink and drown or be strong and swim.

It's not about where I've been. It's about where I'm going. It's not about how I've been playing. It's about how I'm going to play.

I must make sure I focus my attention forward rather than backward. I have let myself down in recent weeks, but I will not let it happen again. Starting today, I will renew my attitude, my enthusiasm, my commitment to going for greatness. I will honor my commitment to playing great.

Focus on Scoring

I am a player. I never let how I am hitting the ball have an impact on how I feel about my ability to get the ball in the hole. I love it when I'm hitting it pure and I love it when the ball isn't going where I'm looking. I take it as a personal challenge and a real source of pride to score when I'm not hitting it well in spite of being diligent and dedicated in practice. These days test my patience but I am strong inside. I hang in there and keep getting the ball up and down until I run out of holes. I see other players who start making up excuses to justify scoring poorly when they are not hitting the ball the way they'd like. But I accept the challenge and patiently wear out the golf course. I stay on my mission of enjoying the challenge of getting the ball in the hole. I believe it is days like these that keep me in tournaments. It is days like these that separate me from others who give in to despair. It is a chance to separate myself from others. I will trust myself and honor my commitment to my talent and myself. I love being strong and patient when others cave in or give in to self-pity. I am focused. I never waver when playing competitively.

Self-Development Exercises

If you're trying to become the best golfer you can be, you'll want to take advantage of every opportunity to develop the mind of a winner. Here are a few mental exercises that can be done by anyone from a Tour professional to someone watching at home. You might want to write down your responses to these questions. They should help you not only to evaluate where you are as a golfer, but to point you in the direction of improvement.

Learn from the Best

Describe the attitudes and behaviors of the most confident players you have ever watched play. Think about their body language—the way they walk, the expressions on their faces. Do their shoulders slump? Do their chins drop? Watch how they go about the game of golf, how they warm up, how they practice, how they respond to all the situations they face. If one of these players is a Tour player and you have a chance to observe him or her in action, concentrate on his or her attitudes and behaviors rather than the score or the position in the tournament. If you can do it, take in a practice day and observe the player's preparatory routine.

Then answer these questions:

- How are these players' behaviors different from yours? Obviously, if you're an amateur, it's likely that they hit the ball farther or straighter. That's not the point. From the time they arrive at the golf course to the time they leave, what are they doing that you're not doing?
- What kind of plan can you put together that can change your attitudes and behaviors and emulate the attitudes and behaviors you find most admirable in the players you've observed?
- Will you honor a commitment to this plan and sustain it until these changes become your habits?

Watch Television Like a Pro

When you watch golf on television, watch from the eyes of a player rather than the eyes of a broadcaster or fan. Mute the sound. Actively engage in the experience as if you were in the lead or in the last group. Put yourself mentally in the picture. How do you think? How do you deal with each situation that arises? This can give you a chance to learn from the experience of others. It's easier than learning the hard way.

Pay particular attention to this exercise during major events, because they get more coverage. You'll see virtually every shot the leaders play, from the first tee to the 18th green.

If you have the equipment, record one of these telecasts. Watch it again with a notebook in your lap. Make a note every time your favorite player misses a fairway, misses a green, or misses a make-able putt. Notice that even the best make mistakes. Rewind and watch yet again, but this time make notes on how your favorite player responds to his or her mistakes. Note how he or she goes about the process of scoring no matter what happens.

Define Yourself

Do you dare to believe that you can be:

> The greatest golfer in your age group?
> The best golfer in your regular foursome?
> The best golfer at your club?
> The best golfer in your club's history?
> The best golfer ever from your city?
> The best golfer ever from your state?
> The best golfer ever from your country?
> The greatest golfer the world has seen?

These are important questions. Take them seriously. Write down your answers. Be truthful with yourself. Every question you answer with a "no" sets a limit on the golfer you can become.

The Thoughts
of Confident Golfers

Confident players develop the ability to monitor and diagnose their golfing thoughts. They become, in effect, their own sports psychologists. They can do this because they know how a confident golfer thinks. Do you?

You may not, because a truly confident golfer can sound cocky, even arrogant when he or she speaks candidly. Such people learn early in their careers that if they express their true feelings, people are going to criticize them. That criticism may stem from jealousy, but it stings nonetheless. So confident players who are also smart players learn to project a façade of modesty and humility to the media and the world. The public doesn't normally get to hear what's really going on in their minds.

I do. Here's a compendium of things I often hear when I talk to players who have their minds in the right place, who are thinking confidently:

- *I don't feel as if I'll ever miss.*
- *I have a feeling of being in complete control. It doesn't matter who is in the field, what others do, or what the course looks like.*

- *I never allow myself to be in awe of anybody else who is human.*
- *It's not only okay to feel pretty cocky on the inside. It's necessary.*
- *I feel like I have an edge that no one else has, whether it's talent, mind, strength, heart, or spirit.*
- *No one can beat me if I play the way I can play.*
- *I respect myself and my game more than I respect anyone else's.*
- *I don't care about scoreboards because I know I am going to win before I tee off.*
- *I'm on top. I set the pace. They have to beat me. I don't have to beat them.*
- *I don't know how to explain it. I just have a feeling that no one can stop me.*
- *I feel that I'll never lose and I'm shocked and surprised when it happens.*
- *I feel euphoric when I'm in the right state of mind.*
- *I'm good and I know it. I don't necessarily show it. I don't tell people about it. But I know they know it.*
- *I sometimes feel so good, I feel sorry for the other players.*
- *I have never been beaten. Sometimes I run out of holes.*
- *Some people think I'm cocky. I'm not. I just think I'm a better golfer than anyone else. At home, I'm really quite down to earth, rather shy and humble.*
- *Sometimes I even amaze myself, but I don't think luck has much to do with it.*
- *Don't ever tell me I can't do something or that something is impossible. If you do, I'll know you don't believe in me the way I believe in myself.*

If you are truly on a mission to discover your potential as a golfer, you'll want to find yourself thinking this way. You must admit that discovering your potential will require a certain swagger when you walk onto a tee, down a fairway, or onto a green to putt. Call it an inner arrogance. Call it your 15th club. It's a feeling that you have an edge on everyone else.

If this feeling comes naturally to you, that's fantastic! Do everything you can to nurture it. Don't let the game beat it out of you.

If these thoughts come hard to you or not at all, accept that you have work to do on your mind. You must do everything possible with your conscious and subconscious minds to develop this kind of attitude and let it fill your mind. Make no mistake about it. You will need this 15th club if you wish to explore your potential.